Wildering

Wildering

ANYONE'S GUIDE TO ENJOYING THE AMERICAN WILDERNESS

Mick Tune

ISBN-13: **9781544819990**
ISBN-10: **1544819994**
Library of Congress Control Number: 2017904621
CreateSpace Independent Publishing Platform
North Charleston, South Carolina

Table of Contents

First Step · 1

My Rules · 7

Where Do I Start? · 12

Choosing a Trail or Route · 18

Choosing a Campsite · 23

Always Have an Old-Fashioned Paper Map · · · · · · · · · · · · · · · 26

Gearing Up for Day Hiking · 27

Gearing Up for Backpacking · 30

Food on the Trail · 42

Weather and Health · 46

Getting There: Airplanes and Travel · · · · · · · · · · · · · · · · · · · 58

Dark Sky · 62

Water · 65

Fire · 70

Mother Nature · 72

About Bears (and Other Creatures) · · · · · · · · · · · · · · · · 73

Kids · 82

Places I Have Pooped · 86

Guns · 90

Planning Ahead for Backcountry Permits in National Parks · · · · · · · 93

Trail Eve and Day · 96

How to Pack Your Backpack · 98

Coming Off the Trail · 101

The People You Will Meet · 103

The Bad Trip (Or Was That a Flying Mountain Goat?) · · · · · · · · · · 111

Tips for the National Park Tourist Trip · · · · · · · · · · · · · · · 115

Resolutions and Knots · 121

Afterword: Environment · 123

About the Author · 125

First Step

---

*In beauty all day long may I walk. Through the
returning seasons, may I walk. On the trail marked with
pollen may I walk. With dew about my feet, may I walk.*

*With beauty before me may I walk. With beauty
behind me may I walk. With beauty below me
may I walk. With beauty above me may I walk.
With beauty all around me may I walk.*

*In old age wandering on a trail of beauty, lively, may
I walk. In old age wandering on a trail of beauty,
living again, may I walk. My words will be beautiful.*
EXCERPT FROM THE CLOSING PRAYER IN THE
NAVAJO WAY BLESSING CEREMONY

am just a guy—and a nearly sixty-year-old guy, at that. I am not Bear
Grylls with a survivalist TV show. I am neither Lewis nor Clark. My
work has no connection whatsoever to the outdoors and requires
practically no physical activity. I am not an Olympian, nor am I any kind
of fitness freak. Even my friends make jokes about my skinny legs. I am
not a professional mountaineer, a former armed-services badass, or a
park ranger. I was never even a Boy Scout. I don't do technical climbing, rappelling, free climbing, or anything that requires specialized
equipment or skills. Physical fitness is certainly an asset to anyone, but

I do not train in some special regimen. I am simply capable of walking. If you are fortunate enough to be physically able and are reasonably healthy, then you are quite capable of being good at walking too.

I have a job and a family and responsibilities that take up most of my life. I cannot spend months at a time on one of those 2,500-mile wilderness trails that people make movies about, but I *can* make time to connect to the much bigger, natural, wilder world. This book is for the recreational/vacation hiker—for the normal sort of person who would like to *enjoy* getting outdoors. If I can enjoy hiking and backpacking, then most of the ambulatory population can explore the astonishing natural wonders of this country. Why the vast majority of Americans rarely takes a significant, off-pavement walk to explore even a fraction of our outdoor treasures is a tragic mystery to me. Fundamentally, walking is the only ability required to enjoy much of the American wilderness.

Upright walking (along with bigger brains and opposable thumbs) is a key ability that distinguishes us as a species. That characteristic helped humans to spread across, adapt to, and conquer the world. From an evolutionary perspective, you and I are built to be *very good* at walking. You will be stunned at how quickly and easily you can become good at walking all day. We are made to walk all day. Walking a lot, or taking a long hike, is not something odd or unnatural; rather, the consistently sedentary lifestyle of most human beings is decidedly unnatural -- a modern, drastic departure from the way we lived for several million years.

Let me give you two examples—a big picture and a local picture—of how walking can radically change your experience and perspective of the country.

A Big Picture

In 2015, over four million people visited Yellowstone National Park—over one million of them during the month of July. (You can find all kinds of park-use stats and reports on the official National Park Service website.) With over one million people in the park in July 2015, only 14,288 backcountry overnight permits were issued. That means that only 0.047 percent of the people who went to Yellowstone in July 2015 walked three miles or more along a well-mapped and maintained trail to pitch a tent and spend a night at a designated backcountry campsite. The statistics only capture the total number of backcountry overnight permits issued for the month, but most backpackers spend more than one night out on a trip. If you assume that the average stay for a backpacker is three nights, then fewer than five thousand people out of the million visitors to Yellowstone in July 2015 managed to walk three or more miles of trail and pitch a tent for an overnight stay. (Blissfully, I was one of those people.) That works out to about 150 people in the backcountry per night that month. Yellowstone comprises about 3,500 squares miles of wilderness—the park is larger than the states of Delaware and Rhode Island combined. So, each night in July 2015, there was one adventurous human being per twenty-three square miles of Yellowstone National Park. In every way, we walkers had a beautiful backcountry to ourselves.

Everyone else (99.95 percent of those one million visitors) was dealing with traffic jams and long lines for concessions. Those visitors were desperately trying to find parking spaces so they could herd themselves from attraction to attraction until the long day was done. Please do not get me wrong; everyone should visit our national parks. Even if you never get out of your car, the parks are definitely worth the trip. Most major national parks are wonderfully set up so that visitors can experience fantastic vistas and stunning natural attractions simply by driving in (or taking a bus) and then navigating a few hundred yards of boardwalk or paved "trail" after finding a place to park. Anyone can—and everyone should—experience these classic "postcard" views of the parks. However, walking a few miles and pitching a tent for the night is an entirely different universe of exploring the real park. Almost anyone can experience that park, too.

A few more statistics will put the experience of walking in perspective. Yellowstone has 466 miles of paved roads. Anyone who has been there can tell you that the park is a really big place that takes days to explore by vehicle/road—even if you are committed to driving all day. The park also has over fifteen miles of boardwalk and paved walking trails for those who wish to get out of their cars, stretch their legs a little, and get a closer view of an attraction. In comparison with these roads and boardwalks, Yellowstone has over a thousand miles of back-country hiking trails. Obviously, only those who are willing to take a walk ever see the wilder majority of Yellowstone's wonders.

I am always surprised at the reaction from the other 99.95 percent of visitors when I am back in civilization (meaning near a road and people) after a few days out on a trail. These conversations typically occur while I am standing in a damn line for a much-anticipated hamburger and beer and trying to acclimate myself to small talk again. I am not prone to starting conversations, and I am not certain why people notice me—maybe because I have not properly bathed in more than a few days. Where did you go? they ask. How did you get there? You walked? With all your stuff?

I am surprised because backpacking is not some great feat or major accomplishment. The experience, the scenery, and the quiet are truly amazing, but there is nothing amazing about backpacking. Literally, all I did was walk, which is not very hard with some sensible planning and preparation. This book is not for the uberhiking crowd, but for the millions of ordinary people like me who are curious about what is around the bend in the bigger, wilder world around them.

A Local Picture

I live in North Texas, in a smallish town near Dallas. Not many people come to Dallas for a wilderness adventure. The topography is flat and boring—and even more so as you continue west. Growing up in Tennessee (hills, mountains, big hardwoods, real rivers), I thought I had moved to some kind of semidesert. What could be interesting—in terms of natural treasures—in a metroplex like Dallas, Texas? Turns out there is quite a lot of interesting stuff. I will bet that there are some fascinating things where you live, too. You will be astounded at what is right under your feet if you just walk awhile and pay attention a little.

Because of a very, very long story of geological processes (sea-level changes, mountain building, uplift, and erosion, just to name a few), much of North Texas has Cretaceous-era rock formations just below the surface soil. Google "Cretaceous" and start exploring: I am not attempting to write a paleontology book. To make an unimaginably long story short, the Cretaceous period, from 125 million to 65 million years ago, was the last great age of the dinosaurs. Dinosaurs get all the press and the movies (and they *are* cool); but then, as now, most of the Earth was ocean. North Texas has some notable Cretaceous-era dinosaur discoveries—the famous shoreline footprints near Glen Rose, the less-famous footprints around Grapevine Lake, and the recently discovered Arlington Archosaur site. When the Dallas/Fort Worth International Airport was built, dinosaur (land-creature) fossils were found on the south side, and marine (ocean) fossils were found on the north side. The airport apparently straddles geological layers where shorelines met sea—or where sea levels receded and rose over long periods. (See *Cretaceous Airport: the Surprising Story of Real Dinosaurs at DFW,* by Louis Jacobs, PhD.) Dinosaur finds are relatively rare in North Texas because in Cretaceous time, the majority of this area was underwater—covered by the great Western Interior Seaway that stretched from the Gulf of Mexico through Texas, Western Kansas, parts of Montana, and Canada, until it met the Arctic Ocean. What North Texas has in abundance is Cretaceous marine fossils—brachiopods, clams, oysters, ammonites, nautiloids, sea turtles, all kinds of fish, abundant sharks, and terrifying marine reptiles such as mosasaurs and plesiosaurs. Find practically any place in North Texas with some erosion—a small hillside, a wash area, a road cut, a stream or river—and the odds are decent that you might pick up a seventy million- to one hundred million-year-old marine fossil. Who would have guessed that with a casual glance at this seemingly boring landscape?

There is a series of creeks about an hour from my home where one can take children to "surface collect" or sift sand for abundant cretaceous shark teeth. I have a handful of large, beautiful ammonites that I chiseled out of a hillside on Sunday afternoons while an access road was being added to the freeway system right in the heart of downtown Fort Worth. There are exposures of fossil-bearing layers in and near downtown Dallas, as well.

Also about an hour's drive from my home is the North Sulphur River, a sparsely populated and rural area. You may not think of the countryside within an hour's drive as the American wilderness, but a good part of that land is still quite wild to most of us. One does not have to be in a designated wilderness area to reconnect with a bit of nature. Hiking around the river, I have encountered bobcats, mountain lions, wild hogs, coyotes, river otters, and beavers—not to mention all manner of snakes, turtles, frogs, salamanders, and spiders. I do not yet have the knowledge to appreciate the many species of birds, plants, and insects in that area.

Most of my regular walking is day hiking around the river. The place is interesting and local. I enjoy the beauty and variety of the always-changing river. As an added benefit, I find marine fossils: mosasaurs, plesiosaurs, Xiphactinuses, sea turtles, ammonites, baculites, shark teeth, and more. The river, usually dry enough for (muddy) walking—but prone to dramatic flashflooding—carves through Cretaceous strata rich in marine fossils.

Why mention all this stuff about fossils in a book about hiking? If you have even moderate brain activity, I believe you will find it impossible to walk out into the world without being curious about what you see around you and learning something about the world right at your feet. Hiking—simply taking a few walks and noticing the surroundings—got me into geology, volcanology, paleontology, archeology, and astronomy (see the chapter titled "Dark Sky"). I have not formally studied any of these things, but I am curious and fascinated—and I still enjoy learning. Maybe you will get into bugs or birds or hydrology or history. Who knows? What I do know is that there is a much bigger (and tinier) and more interesting world out there than you ever imagined.

This book is intended to help you do what 99.9 percent of Americans don't do: get out there a ways! Moreover, this book is intended to help you to *enjoy* that experience. I have no interest in becoming a semicrazed wilderness survivalist; neither, likely, do you. I do, however, love experiencing the American wild that so stunningly few people see. All that fun and discovery requires is being able to walk and to plan. Use your evolutionary advantages; you are good at walking, and you have an unusually large brain. Your opposable thumbs will come in handy, too. You will be amazed at the surprises that you find along the way. The American wild awaits you.

My Rules

The first and most important rule is to **enjoy** getting outside. There is no contest. There is no race. You are not competing for a prize. You have nothing to prove to anyone. There is no medal awarded for reaching a final destination—and that is the point! The point of hiking and backpacking is simply to enjoy the amazing world around you. The point of hiking and backpacking is to get far enough away from your civilized life that you can just enjoy a day in the wild—no schedule, no calls, no beeps. Connect with a world that we have forgotten over the last hundred years.

I have read *A Walk in the Woods* by Bill Bryson. Saw the movie, too. I highly recommend both. The thing that struck me most about the book (the story of a couple of novices who tackle the 2,500-mile Appalachian Trail) was how the author often described the trail and the experience as a daily drudgery. Who wants to do that? Personally, I don't understand long-trail hikers. Bless their hearts, but I don't understand them. I don't understand marathon runners, either. In fact, I don't understand runners. If you ever see me running, then you should probably get moving—something really bad is coming.

Enjoy. Make that experience your primary objective, and you will plan a good trip. You do not have to complete a two thousand-mile trail to have an epic experience. Pack in four miles (in ten hours of daylight, you need only make half a mile an hour and you are good to go), set up a base camp so you don't have to lug a big pack around, spend two days making a couple of fun day hikes with a day pack, and then go home feeling refreshed. After you stretch your trail legs, you can try something a little more challenging. No one, except you, really cares what you do out there. Sit around your base camp all day enjoying the sunshine and a world that does not smell like car exhaust and asphalt. Actually *get away*—from everything. Watch an eagle fish. Make a bow drill for fire starting. Eat fresh-picked huckleberries with your oatmeal. Count stars.

Start with something relatively easy and fun and then grow from there. I am not being naïve; hiking or backpacking does involve some physical exertion. But as I said earlier, you are evolved to walk and will be surprised at how good you can be at walking. No matter what kind of physical shape you are in, carrying a backpack for the first hour or so on a trail is hell. The load and the balance are odd. Your body rebels at something new. But after an hour or two, your body says, "Ah, well... let's move on." The second day is easier than the first day is, and after that, you are officially a backpacker.

Prepare for your trip. Do your homework. Make a plan. You can always change the plan, but that kind of creativity works out much better if you have a solid plan to begin with. Many of the subsequent chapters in this book will help you to do that kind of planning. Research and read everything you can find about the area you are going to. Get a good National Geographic trail map and order a trail guide-book or two for the area. Secure permits or reservations in advance, if needed. Do not overfill your schedule. Everything in your life is rushed; why would you want to rush through this experience? Having some downtime won't hurt you. Know the expected weather conditions and ranges. Have the right equipment and clothes. Make sure that necessities such as water and food are taken care of. Plan a trip that you can enjoy, given your experience and your physical limitations. Make your adventure challenging but realistic. I am somewhat experienced now, but I am getting a bit older; two nights out is fun but too short...more than five nights out is fun but arduous.

Once you are out there, the most important rule is **Don't be stupid**. Recognizing that the range of human stupidity is probably infinite, this book cannot possibly warn you about every dumb thing that could be done. I hope, however, that a few examples and repeating the mantra will drive home the point for you. Don't be stupid. If you need a more positive-sounding rule, how about *Make careful, well-calculated decisions.* Or *Think first—and then think again before acting.*

Every few years, I read about someone stepping off one of the geyser-field boardwalks in Yellowstone National Park (despite a dozen signs reminding people not to do so). Some people walk right up to one of those beautiful, boiling, bottomless, chemical pools (despite all manner of additional warning sings), and fall in when the thin-crust-ground collapses. Those people do not recover; they cook or dissolve or whatever horrible death happens in a soup of boiling, chemical-laced water.

When Mike Sealock (who I will introduce later) and I made the Half Dome summit hike in Yosemite National Park in California, we joked about the multitude of signs (often repeated for nearly a mile above every three-hundred-foot waterfall) telling people to stay out of the river to avoid being swept over the falls. The signs are no joke. Ten people died the summer we were there because they thought that it was a good idea to get in the water above the falls anyway. "Stay Away from the Edge" or "Do Not Proceed Past This Point" signs mean exactly what they say. Such unnecessary injuries and deaths happen in the well-traveled tourist areas of our national parks every year. Don't … be … stupid.

In the backcountry, there are more dangers and no warning signs. There are few people around and there is no infrastructure to help you if you mess up. If no one is around to save you, then you'd better take care of yourself well. Summoning help—much less getting help to you—may be half a day's walk away. Recovering from doing something stupid can be a monumental task in the backcountry.

A simple example: the trail you are on requires a river crossing. You evaluate the river to make sure that it is not too deep or too swift to cross. You scout the shore both ways to see whether, indeed, the best and safest place to cross is right at the trail (likely so). You notice that a huge tree has fallen across the river just downstream. You think, *Why not cross the river by tightrope-walking the tree?. That would be cool.*

Probably fun. I won't have to get in the cold water and all of that. The odds of you injuring yourself if you ford the river the way you are supposed to (taking off your boots and socks, putting on your sturdy water shoes, unbuckling your pack belt, and walking carefully through the water to the other side) are very, very low. You will get wet, but you are not likely to get hurt. The odds of you injuring yourself if you tightrope your little tree-bridge are quite high. The tree is slick. Your boots are wet and muddy. Your pack renders you off-balance, and you are not a circus performer. That trunk has broken branch stubs everywhere, the better to gore you with when you slip. Or the whole thing might just break and fall into the river with you on it. Which option are you going to choose?

Always ask yourself this question (and take the time to think through the answer): *What is the simplest and safest way for me to do what I need to do?* And if you are trying to do something that you don't really need to do, then consider that question a second time. The answer may be that you simply don't need to do it.

A part of being smart (and enjoying your trip) is knowing your limits and the limits of the people walking with you. Push and challenge yourself some, yes; but driving to someone's breaking point does not make for an enjoyable experience. Remember rule number one again; you are not out to prove anything to anyone, you are out to enjoy the outdoors! Stop when anyone needs to. Take long breaks. Enjoy diversions along the way. Help each other out. Reevaluate your plan for the day, if you need to. Maybe the weather is just not right for the day hike you planned. Maybe you need to hunker down for a day or to turn back from that peak. Becoming too exhausted, too cold, too hot, too dehydrated, or too wet leads to mistakes, accidents, or worse.

Thankfully, in more than thirty years of hiking and backpacking, I have not had even a significant minor injury, nor has anyone with me had one. Have we been lucky? Certainly. Accidents can happen to anyone. Mostly, though, we have been careful and sanely thoughtful about self-preservation. We have fun and plenty of adventure. We do plenty of stupid things—such as building an amazingly anatomically correct snowman named Woody, who sat around our campfire pit for days—and stayed there to greet someone else. We do not do stupid things that might get someone hurt.

The last rule is **Be a good guest**. Don't be destructive, loud, or obnoxious. Leave no trash and as little trace of your presence as possible. Follow the rules even if you don't like them. Watch out for others. Be helpful. Be respectful of the wonder of nature around you. In the backcountry, you are the guest—the visitor, not the owner.

Where Do I Start?

*Everyone needs beauty as well as bread, places
to play in and pray in, where nature may heal
and give strength to body and soul alike.*

JOHN MUIR, IN *THE YOSEMITE*

Sure, you should do some research. You can read magazines, articles, and books such as John Muir's *The Yosemite*. However, you will learn best by *doing*.

Despite the popularity of several recent movies, wandering off on a wilderness trail with no experience and no clue about how to proceed or what to expect is an unnecessarily dumb (and likely unpleasant) plan. It's akin to throwing the kid in the lake to see if he can figure out how to swim. You will likely survive; but remember that the first rule is to *enjoy* your experience!

The first backpacking trip I took was with two old guys. (They were probably fifteen years younger than I am now, but at the time, I thought they were ancient.) They were friends of a friend. I had never met either one of them, and I could not tell you their names now. They knew what they were doing, however. Despite all my research, I did not. The lesson? If you really want to learn about something, then hang out with people who already know a lot about that thing.

When I decided to learn something about paleontology, I found a paleontologist (on the Internet—what a world we live in! You can find a way to learn anything you want to) who paid for his summers in the field by selling trips to people like me. I went out in the field with people who knew a lot more than I did, and I learned by doing. Returning home, I found and joined the Dallas Paleontological Society, a wonderful group of professionals and enthusiastic amateurs. I spent time with people who could teach me, help me, and mentor me in a hands-on way. Making interesting new friends was also a blessing. I went to monthly lectures and on field trips. As soon as I was somewhat competent as an amateur paleontologist, I found ways to give back by encouraging others.

Go with someone more experienced on your first wilderness trip— a friend, a friend of a friend, an REI group outing, a backpacking club, whatever. Enjoy some interesting company and learn something. I never went on another group backpacking trip (unless I put the group together), but that first outing helped me to learn a great deal. That first experience gave me some skills and the confidence to explore on my own, setting me on the course of enjoying a lifetime of wilderness experiences.

Start easy and grow. Again, the first rule is to enjoy your experience. Despite the corny messages of movieland, don't tackle the two-thousand-mile Appalachian or Pacific Coast trails on your first outing. Try some long day hikes in your area. Do some camping beside your car (with day hikes to a destination or two) at a state park. Go to an awesome national park or to one of the many national wilderness areas. (They are less crowded and do not require permits in advance.) Go for a couple of nights out instead of for a week. Enjoy a few easy trips, and then challenge yourself more as you gain some experience.

Find a friend for trail trips—or friends, if you are very blessed. Dr. Mike Sealock is that friend for me (and I'll give a shout-out to Beth Cauley, too). Dr. Mike Sealock has been my friend and frequent adventure sidekick for more than twenty-five years. I was there at the hospital when his (now adult) daughters were born. He cares for my "children" too – Mike is the veterinarian to my pets. The Sealocks are, in every sense, family to my wife (Lisa) and to me.

Backpacking is not a solo experience. You might take a long day hike into a wilderness area alone—if you already know the area very well and/or if the trail has good traffic in case you need help. For all kinds of reasons, including basic safety concerns, trail experiences are something you share with someone. I would not have seen, or appreciated, nearly as much of the world if Mike were not my friend. I will always raise a glass of good scotch to him and to all of those companions who have walked a trail with me. I sincerely hope we will take a trail year after year until we have no more years left.

Beth Cauley, who was an elder at my church, is another trail friend. Her late husband, Pat, was a good friend too. Tragically, he died of amyotrophic lateral sclerosis (ALS). For four years, Beth, a nurse, nursed him. For his last two years, our church set up a schedule of people to spend the day with Pat so Beth could work and support their family. For the last year, I was there almost every day because I could pick him up and move him. I loved Pat. I loved the church that cared for Pat as best it could. I love Beth and her daughters. They are family to my wife, to the Sealocks, and to me. Beth is a trooper. She took whatever shit life threw at her and raised two awesome daughters. She stood by me even when I did not deserve it. For many years, she was a part of our backpacking trips. Sometimes her daughters and their friends joined us too. Always good to have a nurse (Beth) and a doctor (Mike—veterinarians are the best) around. Priceless to have real friends around. By the way, one of Beth's daughters, Jana, would soon kick my butt at any outdoor adventure imaginable. Bear Grylls is a cartoon character to her—he would be a rest-break snack on her agenda. If this book ever has a second edition, she will be the one who makes it better.

The year after Pat died, Beth was with a group of us on a backpacking trip in the Pecos Wilderness. On the first night out, we had a stunning evening of stargazing in a broad alpine meadow beside our campsite (see the "Dark Sky" chapter). Very late that night—actually, early in the morning, my wife and I heard the longest, most blood-curdling scream imaginable and shot bolt upright from deep sleep. It sounded like a woman was being horribly murdered somewhere nearby.

"What...was...that?" Lisa asked me.

My inherent Male Answer Syndrome usually provides a plausible-sounding response even when I am completely inventing an answer. This time, I paused awhile. "I think it was a big cat. Maybe made a kill." (I am pretty sure that I was right.)

"Oh," she said. There was nothing else to say. It was so dark that we could not see each other in the small, two-person tent. I was not about to go out to investigate. We lay down, heard nothing else at all for a while, and went back to sleep. The next morning, at coffee and breakfast around the fire ring, our entire group was talking about that sound. What was it? We eventually agreed on the big cat theory. Beth got to breakfast later, after sleeping longer. Somehow, she had heard nothing at all. Later, she told me that the night was the first good sleep she'd had in four years. The trail can be a healing place.

One of our best group trips did not include backpacking at all. Our little walking company went to Hawaii, stood on a cliff one evening with the sun setting and the waves crashing in, and married Beth to a good man, Mr. Mike Voss. The world keeps turning, and life rolls on. Good things happen too.

Back to topic, let me repeat that staying in the backcountry should not be a solo experience. Any little issue or accident can be a major, life-threatening problem if you are alone. Help is not likely to arrive anytime soon. Passersby are few, if any.

On a recent backpacking trip in Yellowstone, I (inadvertently) spent a couple of nights somewhat alone. Despite being experienced and comfortable in the backcountry, I surprisingly and quickly became uneasy. Mike, his daughter Julia, and my younger brother's (Scott) son Hap, and I had planned the trip and put in for the necessary back-country permits months in advance. At the last moment, my brother was also able to join us. This trip was the first significant backpacking experience for Julia, Scott and Hap. We were excited, but we now had five people and a designated campsite permit for only four people. Fortunately, I was able to procure a last-minute permit from the ranger station for one person at a nearby campsite. One site was number four on the lake, and the other was number five (a handful of designated campsites are sometimes clustered around destinations on backcoun-try trails). I was not going to split up Mike and his daughter or Scott and his son, so I took the spare site. We thought the campsites would be close together, but "nearby," as we learned, is a relative term. We walked in almost ten miles to a beautiful mountain lake. Not a single person was on the lake or around it when we arrived. The lake was huge. One of the tallest peaks in Yellowstone loomed over the quiet waters. Our small company left me at the side trail to campsite number four, assuming that site number five would be a few hundred yards or so along the main trail.

I walked down to a gorgeous campsite tucked into the woods right off the shore of the lake. Two tents were permissible there, but I was the only person around. I unloaded my backpack, set up my tent, and got everything organized for the evening and the next day. As I walked around a bit to see the late-afternoon sun on the lake and on the mountain peaks, I thought, *What a great trip this is going to be!* I wondered why I did not hear any sound of the rest of my party setting up camp nearby. I put all of my food (except dinner) in a bag tied with a thirty-foot rope and then found the campsite's bear-pole contraption (see the chapter "About Bears"). My first a-little-something-to-think -about moment was when I noticed the huge (really, very huge), deep, and quite fresh claw marks on the bear pole's vertical support tim-ber. Apparently, the local population knew well where to find treats. Bear poles and food-prep areas are intentionally set up "away" from campsites—but we are talking several hundred feet, maybe. I could have heard those claw marks being made from my tent.

My next something-to-think-about moment came as I headed down the main trail to join my companions for dinner at their campsite. I walked and walked and walked some more. I turned back briefly, think-ing that surely I had missed the little wooden sign marking the side trail to their campsite. I had not. So, I kept walking. I finally found them at campsite number five, much more than a mile from my campsite—not the kind of next-door arrangement we had assumed. We ate dinner, visited, and planned the next day. I was anxious to get back on the trail to my tent. I did not want to be walking a mile and a half alone, in the dark, with big bear claws nearby. That early evening is the only time I have ever (speed) walked a trail with bear spray unholstered, unlocked, and in my left hand, ready to fire. At my tent, more than a mile away from anyone, dark fell quickly. There was nothing to do but get in the bag and go to sleep. I usually enjoy listening to the amazing quiet as dark descends…and then to the emerging sounds of a forest before I sleep. But that night, every sound made my heartbeat quicken just a little. I made myself chill out, but that was something I had never had to do before. It's funny; I have no illusions that Sealock's snores or flatulence would drive away a bear, but something about having another person within shouting distance is comforting.

The morning sun woke me up to a chilly, spectacular day. I was glad to find my food bag hanging undisturbed from the bear pole. While unpacking breakfast and coffee, I realized I had given my matches to Scott the night before. Crap. Cold breakfast and no warm coffee.

We had a fantastic day of fishing, swimming, exploring some nearby thermal features, and hiking. By that night, I had gotten much more comfortable with the solitude at my campsite. That is, until well after dark, I heard lots of heavy trampling very close to my tent and coming in my direction. I quickly put boots on. With my knife in one hand and my bear spray in the other hand, I quietly slipped outside and behind my tent. I tried to be invisible and ready at the same time. Suddenly, a light flashed across my face, and a woman screamed.

A young couple had arrived (despite the triple bad planning of getting on the trail late, not realizing how long the trail was, and having to keep walking well after dark) with a permit for the other tent site. I scared them much worse than they scared me. I stepped out from behind the tent and apologized for startling them. Abruptly realizing that I was wearing nothing but socks, boots, and travel underwear sold with the advertisement that you can wear it for a month at a time, I apologized again. I reminded them to hang their food on the bear pole, and promptly retired to my tent. I thought about helping them set up their campsite as a good neighbor, but then I figured that they had probably already seen quite enough of me for the evening. I slept well the rest of night and had hot coffee waiting for them at the fire pit in the morning, where we more properly introduced ourselves.

Choosing a Trail or Route

Keep the basic rules/questions in mind. What would you enjoy? What are your limitations and the limitations of your group? Some other questions are important, too. How much time do you have? What would you like to see or find?

Start by exploring your local area and/or nearby state parks. Plan some half-day hikes. Practice camping beside your car.

When you are ready to explore a national park, national forest, or federal wilderness area, then get several good trail books about the area (Falcon Guides or other resources) that describe each trail and provide directions, trail markers, distance, difficulty level, and notable sights in detail. When you hit the trail, you don't have to carry the whole book—just photocopy the germane pages. Do some Internet research. Get a good trail map; the National Geographic Trails Illustrated Series is excellent. Pick the trails you would like to travel and a couple of alternate options.

Trails graded "easy" and "moderate" should be fair game. Trails are graded "strenuous" sometimes for their sheer length, but more often the grade refers to steep ascents and/or to multiple ascents and descents. Walking up a mountain or out of a canyon does require some physical exertion. So does slogging through knee-deep mud in a flat river where you are looking for fossils.

For day hiking, with breaks and plenty of time for sauntering and enjoying and picture taking, figure on making a mile every thirty minutes. For backpacking, figure an hour per mile.

Add an hour for a long lunch and an hour or two for exploring a site of interest. I am not interested in speed records. I am out there to enjoy the place and the pace.

Day Hiking

Your physical limits will determine the options here. You can carry enough water for most partial-day hikes, although I strongly encourage carrying a water-purification device and planning a route along which you know you can replenish your drinking water supply if you are going to be out for more than half a day. Many national parks have iconic, full-day hikes, such as the Half Dome summit hike in Yosemite, the Hanging Gardens and Highline Trail above Going to the Sun Road in Glacier National Park, the Narrows or Angel's Landing in Zion National Park, the Devils Garden in Arches National Park, the Hoh River Trail in Olympic National Park, the Cascade Canyon Trail in Grand Teton National Park, and the Elephant Canyon trail in Canyonlands National Park.

You can also have a fantastic day in any national park by taking two or three shorter hikes. Generally, day hikes do not require any kind of permit—the Half Dome summit in Yosemite is the only hike I am aware of that now requires a permit. The more famous trails are somewhat heavily used. Parking is limited. A big tip: start early for a long hike. Get to the trailhead at daylight or shortly after, and you will enjoy most of your hike with very few other people around. Use a park bus system to get around when you can. Many of the best days I have had outdoors were well-planned day hikes.

When we took the Half Dome hike in Yosemite, Sealock and I got to the trailhead before 7:00 a.m. It was nine relentlessly uphill miles with five thousand feet of elevation gain and nine miles back, plus nearly another mile to the parking area. We did not get back to the car until well after dark. I distinctly remember smelling and then spotting a hot dog stand on the walk from the trailhead to the parking lot. Let's say the hot dog stand closed at 9:00 p.m. We walked up at 9:02 p.m. I was salivating, ready to eat a dozen hot dogs. I went to the window and asked the guy how much for four hot dogs.

"We are closed," he replied. Literally, he was throwing away left-over hot dogs while I watched.

"What would it take for me to buy those hot dogs you are throwing away?" I asked.

"We are closed," he said, and he shut the wooden window in my face. We had more than an hour's drive back to where we were staying. All I could think of the whole way were hot dogs.

When we took the Highline Trail in Glacier National Park, hiking nearly fourteen miles from the top of Logan Pass, past the Granite Chalet, and down to the midway curve on Going to the Sun Road, Sealock and I got another early start. We parked in the ample lot at the park's bus center and caught the first express bus to the top of Logan Pass. The views were stunning for the entire day; truly, we were walking the rim of the "crown of the continent." When we finished the trail at Going to the Sun Road late that afternoon, we simply hopped on a bus and rode back to the transportation center and our car.

By the way, Sealock and I were both well into our fifties when we took those two epic day hikes. You do not have to be an Olympic athlete to tackle a challenging day hike. Just give yourself plenty of time to enjoy the day.

If I only have a day or two at an interesting location, then I will plan a shorter hike (or two or three) for each day. Do some research to make the most of your day. Go to the trailhead farthest from where you are staying early in the morning and then work your way back. I saw a stunning variety of ecosystems in Olympic National Park on the back end of a business trip just by looking at a map and planning well. Someday, I hope to go back for a much longer walk.

Recently, with Sealock, his daughter Julia, and my nephew Hap, we planned an entire weeklong trip around day hiking. My nephew had never been to Glacier National Park, and I wanted him to see as much of the park as possible. Backpacking is awesome, but you are limited to the one small area that you walk into. With a day-hiking strategy, we would experience a much wider variety of the park's scenery. We took our tents and drove around inside the park the first afternoon until we found a public campsite that was open; twenty dollars a night is a helluva deal, but you cannot make reservations. We planned four full days of day hikes—two full-day hikes and two days of multiple hikes—but we did not care which order we did them in. We could adjust our plan according to weather or opportunity. We wanted to stay a night at the Granite Chalet along the Highline Trail, but reservations are practically impossible to get, even a year in advance. Our flexible schedule was designed so that if we discovered that the chalet had availability due to cancellations, we could jump on the opportunity.

Backpacking

One of the best backpacking trips I have ever taken started at Old Faithful in Yellowstone, continued over the Continental Divide, and then followed the Bechler River from its headwaters to a ranger station in the state of Idaho. We saw so many gorgeous waterfalls that by day three we were jaded. *Oh, yeah...another spectacular waterfall.* Fun trip, but we did have to carry heavy packs every day and make/break camp every day. We also had to plan transportation carefully because our end point in Idaho was many, many miles (by road) from our starting point in Wyoming. Mike had left one of the rental cars at the end point, but the car was far too small for our whole group and all of our gear. I ended up hitching a ride back to the center of Yellowstone.

Take it easy on your first backpacking trip. Look for a trail that is less than five miles to your campsite. A six- or seven-mile hike is a normal backpacking day; covering eight to ten miles is working quite hard. Anything longer than ten miles a day with a backpack is not a trip I consider enjoyable. Try planning a backpacking trip in which you establish a base camp for several days and then take day hikes from that camp to other points of interest. You will appreciate a couple of days of challenging day hiking after carrying a big pack for six to ten miles. Plus, coming back to home-sweet-home base camp without a bunch of set up to do just feels good. Remember rule number one: *enjoy!*

On a backpacking trip, access to reliable places to replenish water is critical, and camping very near a water source is an essential convenience.

Any backpacking trip requires some intentional, advance planning. Staying in the backcountry of most national parks requires designing an itinerary, choosing designated campsites, and acquiring permits from the park rangers. Later chapters in this book will help you to navigate that planning and permitting process.

By the way, *stay on the trail*. Losing the trail is not a good thing. Do not invent shortcuts. Trail systems are well planned and will be your best route. Staying on the trail means that you do not haphazardly trample and kill all kinds of delicate flora and fauna. More importantly, the trail keeps you from being lost. If you are already capable of navigating wilderness areas with no trails by using a map and a compass, then you do not need to bother reading the rest of this book. If you are like the rest of us—99.99 percent of the population—then when you leave the trail to explore some (very close by) area of interest, *be sure that you know exactly how to reacquire the trail*. In a wilderness area, the trail is your buddy. Always know exactly where your buddy is.

Choosing a Campsite

B e aware of the rules in the national park, federal wilderness area, national forest, state park, or private land you plan to camp on. Some areas, like most national parks, have a permitting process and require a planned itinerary for specific backcountry campsites. Some areas require no permits, reservations, or planned itineraries, but still encourage you to use only existing campsite areas. Some areas have few regulations at all. Google the area you are visiting to find the entity that manages those lands; the website of that management entity will provide the regulations for camping. (See the chapter titled "Planning Ahead for Backcountry Permits in National Parks.")

If you are camping in an area with few (or no) regulations, at least observe the following rules of etiquette:

- Even if permits, planned itineraries, and designated campsites are not required, let someone know where you are going, where you hope to be each day, and when you expect to exit. Make sure a family member has a copy of your expected itinerary. Share that plan with a nearby ranger station you stop at for information. Cell phones do not work in these places. If someone needed to find you, or if you went missing for a day or more, then the information you left with someone could be very important in tracking you down.
- Even if you are free to camp "anywhere," make every effort to find an already used and trampled campsite and fire ring.

There is no sense in trampling more of this wilderness area for another campsite when you can avoid it.

- If possible (and permissible by regulations), make your camp near a reliable water source. You need access to water that you can purify for cooking, cleaning, and replenishing your drinking supply.
- Most areas will regulate how close to a water source you may camp. These regulations exist for important reasons. Campsites create damage and erosion, which can disrupt streams and watersheds. Your food, trash, excrement, and urine are not welcome close to watersheds, either. Wildlife still needs access to that water too. There is an important safety issue, as well; many rivers, creeks, watersheds, and lakes flood quickly and drastically if there is rain. Make camp a hundred yards or more from the water source—and on higher ground.
- For lightning protection, camp just inside in a wooded area, preferably in a cluster of smaller trees surrounded by larger trees. Camping in an open field or meadow, especially at higher elevation, puts you at significant lightning-strike risk.
- For tent space, find a level area free of shrubs and debris. Clear out sticks and rocks that would be under your tent's footprint. Set up your tent so that you have a clear path to get in and out. If the ground is not quite level, orient the tent so that your head, when you are sleeping, is on the higher side.
- Set up your food and fire ring area for cooking and eating a hundred feet or more from the tent sites. Use an existing fire ring where you can. See the chapter titled "Fire" if you need to build a fire ring. Do not make a fire in this area if there is a fire ban in effect! If fires are permissible, use only already downed wood for fuel. Do not make a fire in windy conditions. Keep your fire small and under control. Make double sure that your fire is completely out when you are finished. Do all of your cooking, cleaning, and eating in this spot. Bag and hang all of your trash and food near this area.
- If you are in bear country, then definitely bag and hang all of your food and trash with the bear pole method. (See the chapter

titled "About Bears.") Even if you are not in bear country, food and trash attract all kinds of critters and bugs. Bagging and hanging your food from a tree limb well above your reach is a good practice to keep your campsite clean and free of pests.

- Consider planning a trip in which you set up a base camp and then take several days of day hikes from that camp location. The benefits of that kind of planning are awesome. You do not have to carry a heavy backpack every day. You do not have to break down, pack, then later unpack and set up camp every day. When you get back from a long day of hiking and exploring, camp is already set up and waiting for you.

Always Have an Old-Fashioned Paper Map

read news stories every year about people who wander off on some hike and become hopelessly lost. They either accidently find a road a day or two later or have to be rescued because (somehow, to their surprise) their phone had no signal, their app would not work, or their gizmo ran out of batteries or was dropped and broken.

Buy—and learn to read and use—an old-fashioned, paper, topographic trail map. Learn how to use a simple compass. Technology is not a reliable friend in the wilderness, but a good, paper trail map will never let you down. Take technology on the hike as your splurge item if you wish to (and enjoy playing with those toys), but *rely on* a good, paper trail map. Besides, a real map is lighter and easier to carry around than electronics with batteries or solar-power attachments are. Part of the fun of hiking is spreading out a map and talking about where you are and where you are going.

The National Geographic Society sells excellent waterproof and practically indestructible topographical trail maps (in the Trails Illustrated series) for almost any place you might go in the United States. Keep a real trail map with you at all times, even on a day hike.

Gearing Up for Day Hiking

B uy a high-quality, durable, spacious day pack. The Ninja Turtles "backpack" your kids take to school is not a good option. You want some real padding on the shoulder straps. You also want a waist belt to cinch. Always look for an assortment of zipper entrances, pockets, and mesh side pockets for water bottles.

The Thing about Shoes

I am always surprised on day-hiking trails to see people wearing flip-flops, loafers, cheap tennis shoes, or plastic contraptions. Whatever the weather might be (even if it is quite hot), please wear real shoes/boots and socks meant for the rigors of hiking. You will stub your toes hard about a hundred times a day on a backcountry trail. Blisters from crappy shoes or failing to wear socks make for a bad day. Tired, bruised feet are not happy feet. The ground often changes from wet to dry to muddy to very hard and rocky to gritty to marshy. Your kids *should be* whiny if you are making them walk several miles in cheap, horrible, plastic shoes. If you are going to walk very far on any almost any trail, then wear thick, shock-absorbing hiking socks and mostly waterproof, high-top hiking boots.

What to Carry and Wear

Do not go on a long day hike without the ability to replenish and purify water. When Mike and I did the iconic (and very long) Half Dome summit hike in Yosemite, we were stunned by how many unprepared, thirsty hikers we met on the trail. That hike is more than eighteen miles, half of which is uphill. (Ever since that hike, whenever Sealock and I are tired on a trail, we look at each other, and one of us says, "Well, it's not Half Dome.") The first half of the ascent follows a raging river up and over three towering waterfalls. At the halfway point, the trail leaves the river and is bone dry for the rest of the hike. That spot on the river is the last water source on the trail. Many hikers we met there had already consumed the water in their two puny plastic bottles. They had no water-purifying system to replenish at the river, and they still had four hard miles up and then nine miles back before they got more drinking water.

Wear light, loose clothing made of breathable fabric. Even in hot weather, I often wear long (zip-off) pants and a long-sleeved shirt. The long clothes keep bugs and scratchy undergrowth off me and provide sunburn protection. I can always zip off the pant legs and roll up the sleeves if I wish to. If you will be in an area known for wide temperature ranges and rapidly changing weather, or if you will be gaining altitude, then be sure to carry some warmer layers. Weather can change quickly, especially in mountainous areas. The temperature will decrease significantly and the wind will increase significantly if you are gaining altitude. Bring a heavier long-sleeve shirt and a pullover or jacket with a hood. Bring rain gear (which can also act as a windbreaker and an extra layer of warmth.) Carry an extra pair of socks—and water shoes and swimwear if you plan to cross rivers or swim.

Have fun with a delicious picnic! Food choices are nearly unlimited—as long as nothing needs to be cooked or will spoil within eight hours. Because you are only going to be out for a day, you can take a variety of fresh foods such as fruits and breads. Pack some food items that are high in calories and protein and easy to snack on.

Below is the complete list of things that I recommend carrying on your person or in your day pack:

- map
- water purifying system and two water containers
- camera

- sunglasses
- knife
- sunscreen
- bug spray
- matches and/or lighter
- hat
- small flashlight or headlamp
- backpacking towel if you plan on river crossings or swimming
- small binoculars
- pared-down first aid supplies
- bear spray if you are in bear country
- fishing equipment if your destination and interests warrant it
- extra clothing that can be layered for warmth: rain gear, long shirt and pants, pullover or jacket
- food
- your little poop shovel and a roll of biodegradable toilet paper
- special equipment for fossil hunting, photography, or to accomplish other objectives

Gearing Up for Backpacking

You may carry all sorts of things on your excursion; the thing to understand is that *you will be carrying all of that stuff* all day long, every day. There is no luggage service. Your back is the overhead bin space. The goal is to be properly prepared while carrying as little weight as possible. You would prefer to get your fully-loaded backpack into the forty-pound range, but the fifty-pound range is acceptable. If you are carrying more than sixty pounds, re-evaluate your load. In my younger days, despite my skinny legs, I was a renowned pack mule. I could pack all kinds of extra stuff and take on half of your load, too. In my own head movies—in which I refuse to recognize aging—I still think I can do that. But I am not foolish enough to try. The more often you go backpacking, the lighter your backpack will become.

There is a sensible limit to how little you should carry, however. Being in the backcountry without proper clothing for changing weather, without water filtration, without enough food, without a good tent and rain gear, and so on is…well…dumb.

Personal Equipment
Tent
Spend some money; you are going to be living in there. Buy a high-quality, two- or three-season, two-person backpacking tent. Recreational backpacking is done mostly in the summer months, so you do not need a tent that could protect you on Mount Everest. Be

sure that the tent comes with (or purchase extra) a rainfly and a ground cover. *Your tent must stay dry*, hence the absolute necessity of a rainfly. The groundcover (almost any cheap thing will do as long as it is very light and the right size) helps to avoid moisture and protects your tent floor. You can also use the groundcover as an emergency rain tarp, if needed.

Why carry a two-person tent when lighter, one-person tents are available? Well, you may have someone sleeping with you. Personally, I will carry the extra weight of a two-person tent just for my own use. I like having some space. I like having room to keep other things dry inside my tent. However, when you are with another person or a group, and someone's tent is waterlogged or is otherwise a bust, then you can easily adjust and accommodate if you have a two-person tent. Pay attention to the weight and the size of the tent when it is packed up—this thing will be strapped to your pack for every step on the trail. You are looking for a tent that is durable, as light as possible, and easy to set up.

Sleeping Bag

Again, spend some money here. If the weather turns nasty cold (or even snowy), your bag and your tent are your safe refuge. The Scooby Do-themed bag is not going to work. Get a sleeping bag rated to twenty degrees Fahrenheit—the temperature can drop below freezing in the mountains, even on midsummer nights. Pay attention to the size of the bag when it is packed up—a big, fluffy, bulky item will take up too much room in your backpack.

Sleeping Pad and Pillow

You will want some kind of sleeping pad. Therm-a-Rest pads (and other brands) pack well and work reasonably well. Do not get some giant air mattress, or something that is not durable and rugged. Various items sold as backpacking "pillows" are terrible as well as a waste of space and weight. Stuff most of the clothes you are not wearing into an old stuff sack and then wrap your soft fleece outerwear around that sack.

Presto! You made a great pillow. As a bonus, your warm fleece and clothes are right there if you need to get up and go to the bathroom during the night.

Backpack

I don't think they even make the old, external-frame backpacks I used to carry anymore. Today, every pack, including mine, has a (much better!) internal frame. Your pack should last for more than a decade, so choose judiciously. Any good outfitting retailer such as REI will be able to help you with the proper fit. I prefer Kelty packs, but other good brands are available. If you are a bit skinny as I am, be sure the belt cinches tightly enough to sit upon your (nonexistent) hips and butt. A backpack should shift weight onto your hips and legs (through the belt connection above your hips and butt) rather than strain your shoulder straps. Most modern packs have fancy hydration systems with internal bladders and tubes so you can suck in a little water anytime while walking down the trail. I don't care much for that feature—which probably just makes me an old fart. All the trouble of removing bladders and getting purified water into them seems like a hassle to me, so I just carry water containers. I also don't like the idea of having a bladder full of water right next to all of the stuff I am trying to keep dry. Do whatever you wish. Unless you aspire to be a pack mule (not recommended), you do not need the largest-capacity pack ever made. You do, however, want as many side pockets, entry zippers, and compartments as you can get.

Day Pack

Well-planned backpacking trips often include establishing a base camp and then taking several long day hikes from that camp. For those day hikes, you might choose to take a day pack. Most modern backpacks include detachable tops to use for day hiking, but those features are usually little more than fancy fanny packs that can carry a little food and water for a half-day jaunt but do not have enough space for extra layers and rain gear, fishing equipment, etc. Make your own judgment here. If I am planning a trip that includes long day hikes from a base camp, then I attach a day pack to my backpack. Of course, you could empty your backpack of everything but what you need for that day and head on out. Make sure that your day pack has some kind of belt cinch to keep from wearing out your shoulders on a long hike. Multiple compartments are always a plus.

Water Containers and Filtration

Water is heavy, but take at least two, full, durable, thirty-two-ounce water containers per person. I always carry three—being thirsty is not something I enjoy. Besides, someone else in the group almost always runs out of water. Be sure that one of your water bottles has visible measurements in ounces—you will need that information for preparing freeze-dried meals.

A good water-filtration system is an absolute necessity, even if you are just day hiking. There are all kinds of products on the market now. The old iodine pills work, but the water tastes awful, and you have to wait thirty minutes before drinking it. Get a tried-and-true hand-pump system that is easy to carry, easy to clean, and durable. The one I have has lasted more than ten years. You can pump a mudhole and get clean water if you have to. Hand pump systems force water through a filtering cylinder which removes debris and harmful organisms. Of course, if you were to actually pump muddy water, then you will clog the filtering system much faster – requiring you to disassemble and clean (abrasively scrub) the filtering cylinder. Disassembly, cleaning, and assembly are simple tasks. Whenever you notice that your hand pump system requires more physical force to process water, then it is time to disassemble and clean your tool. A lot of the new technology in water purification looks flimsy and fragile to me—besides requiring filter changes and/or batteries. I see no need to upgrade what works for me.

Carry one large, light, collapsible water container for every four people in your group. A collapsible bucket or a large bladder that you can hang will do. Fill that container when you make camp. Accessing water without having to walk all the way down to the water source is a great convenience.

One early afternoon at a backcountry campsite on the upper Quartz Lake in Glacier National Park, I was hanging out on the lakeshore when a young couple arrived. Mike and I had been backpacking and camping for several days, but people who wanted to see the beautiful lake and then return to civilization sometimes used the trail for long day hikes. I introduced myself to the young couple, sat down on a log beside the lake, and engaged in some small talk. I noticed that they were not using their down time to eat anything or to drink water. I saw only one water bottle in each of their day packs, and they were empty. The walk to this lake was six miles or more up, over, and then down a mountain range. They still had to walk out six miles before their day was finished. We talked awhile.

"You don't have any water, do you?" I finally said.

"No," the guy sheepishly responded. "The trail in was a little longer than we thought...and we got thirsty coming over the high ridge."

I retrieved my water-purifying hand pump and made the kid pump as much water as they could stand to drink. Then they filled their two water bottles.

"I should get one of those," he said.

"Yes," I affirmed, "you absolutely should if you ever want to do something like this again."

Kitchen

Get a set of light, nested, titanium cookware with two pots and one pan (you may have to buy the small frypan separately). If you have more than three people in your party, then bring another set of cookware. I have cooked meals over a campfire with an old coffee can and a piece of grill grate, but a small gas stove is much easier, quicker, lighter, and more efficient. The Pocket Rocket gas stove for backpacking is small, weighs nearly nothing, and works fantastically well. Camp stove gas cannot be carried or checked in luggage on a plane, so you may need to purchase this item near your destination.

Always carry two stoves within the group; I have never had one malfunction, but being without a working cookstove would be bad news. Besides, if more than two people are on your trip, an extra stove to keep hot water available is great. Remember that you cannot carry camp stove gas, matches, fire starters, etc. on an airplane, so you will need to plan to buy those important items before hitting the trail. Make sure your pots have lids. They make liquid boil faster and stay warm longer, and they keep debris out. Carry a pot gripper—those pots get hot! Put a little cooking oil in a small vial. Carry some spices, if you wish, but repackage them into the smallest, lightest containers you can find. Bring a bit of folded-up aluminum foil, as well. For utensils, all you need to eat with is a lightweight spork (you already have a knife with you). I carry two stainless-steel Sierra cups—one deep and tall to put hot drinks in and one wider and shallow to put food in. You do not need plates or bowls or blah, blah, blah. As for cooking utensils, a sawed-off wooden spoon and the littlest (maybe also sawed-off) lightweight spatula will do. Foldable utensils are great because you can pack them into the empty spaces in your pot set. Bring a small scrubber to clean with.

Lights

One per person is enough. Look for small, lightweight, and powerful lights. Headlamps are the best way to go. Be sure to bring an extra set of batteries.

Walking Stick/Poles

Trekking poles are popular, but they are a personal choice. I carry one trekking pole because I find it to be a useful tool (especially for river crossings and for testing water, mud, or snow depth). I've often seen people walking with two poles, but I never do so—I am not cross-country skiing. Half of the time, I am not using the one pole anyway. Of course, you can always have fun making a walking stick from a downed branch you find.

Bear Spray

Every person (but not children) should carry bear spray if you are in bear country. Buy a holster to attach to your belt so the canister is easily accessible to you. Bear spray stashed in the bottom of your pack is not going to do you any good. Bear spray cannot be carried or checked in luggage on a plane, so you may need to purchase this item near your destination.

All-Camp Equipment
Many items might be useful, but you only need one of them for the whole camp group. For example, a fancy Leatherman tool *might* prove useful, but not all four people on your trip need to carry one. Here are some items that someone in the group should carry:

- a good trail map of the area and trail information
- foldable trowels—one for every two people—for burying poop (U-Dig-It makes a great one with a convenient belt attachment)
- one light, folded tarp (with eyelets) per three or four people
- one foldable wood saw
- cookware, stoves, gas (see the kitchen section above)
- a large water bladder or collapsible bucket
- a first-aid kit—the premade kits sold at most outfitting stores offer the advantages of in-date supplies in a handy, well-packed carrying case with a set of instructions and best practices
- gas lantern/light—we used to carry one of these all the time, but we quit because we really did not use it often
- a tent-patching kit
- roll of duct tape
- superglue
- binoculars—not everyone needs a pair, but scanning for wildlife at the far edge of a meadow or watching an eagle soar is fun

Other Personal Items
I always carry the items listed below. I suggest that each person on your trip also have the following:

- water-purification apparatus—at least one rig for every two people
- two knives—a larger locking blade and a Swiss Army pocketknife
- Any medication you regularly use or often need
- unscented sunscreen and lip balm—your face, nose, and ears will sunburn quickly at higher altitudes
- small rolls of biodegradable toilet paper
- matches and/or a lighter—have two reliable ways to make fire
- moleskin (unattended foot blisters will ruin your trip!)
- bug spray or lotion—buy the strongest DEET product you can find; using orange oil or garlic or whatever natural remedy will make you feel great about your holistic choice right up to the point that you are eaten alive by mosquitoes, horse flies, ticks, and midges
- ziplock bags in various sizes, including at least one extra-large one for trash
- several large, heavy-duty trash bags will have a multitude of uses such as hanging and waterproofing your food at night or making a waterproof cover for your backpack or a ground cover
- twenty to thirty feet of rope (for tying tarps and hanging food—not heavy rope for climbing)
- sunglasses
- a whistle in case you get lost or need to make a lot of noise to confuse an animal
- baseball cap/hat
- a small camera with a big memory card—some people use their phones, but the problem is battery life, and there is no phone signal in 99 percent of wilderness areas
- a watch—I like having a waterproof watch, but it's up to you
- a high-absorbency backpacking towel
- bandanna(s) have a plethora of uses—as bandages, sweat rags, handkerchiefs, place mats, and to cover your disgusting hair
- carabineer clips and small bungee straps for attaching things to your pack
- small bottle of camp soap

Personal Hygiene Products
Personally, I just don't bother with this stuff on the trail. You may not bathe for four or five days. Get over yourself. You can take a toothbrush and toothpaste, but bears love the strong smell and taste of toothpaste! All I carry are a comb and a few toothpicks.

As you can tell already, there is a lot of stuff to be ported on your back for a backpacking trip—and we have not covered clothing and food yet.

Clothing
Poor-quality or inadequate clothing will quickly ruin your trip. Get high-quality, durable, breathable fabrics that dry quickly. Learn to layer for changing weather conditions.

Shoes
Spend some money to get high-quality, durable, waterproof-as-possible hiking boots. You are going to be walking all day long over all kinds of terrain and maybe through muck and rain, so the quality of your shoes and socks makes a huge difference. On a recent trip, we had to use all of our duct tape (before we walked even five miles) to try to hold together someone's crappy shoes. Not good. Also carry some well-constructed water shoes with thick soles and treads as well as toe protection. You will need those water shoes for river crossings, swimming, and fishing. Moreover, a solid pair of water shoes gets you out of your hiking boots for the evening. In an emergency, if your hiking boots blow out, the water shoes should be solid enough to get you home.

Socks
Take thick, warm, hiking socks for comfort. Have at least one pair of good socks for every two days on the trail. Wear your clean pair of socks one day while your used pair dries. If you are day hiking, always carry a pair of extra socks—it's great to put on dry socks if you get unintentionally soaked.

Underwear

A couple pairs will do; more is a personal preference. I buy those durable, travel underwear that advertise that two pairs will last for a several-month trip. They are easy to wash in a creek, quick to dry, and comfortable. They also work as a swimsuit.

Long Underwear

Yes, summer nights and early mornings in the mountains can be very cold. Long underwear is a lightweight, excellent underlayer for colder weather—and it makes for comfortable trail jammies, too.

Pants

I prefer pants with zip-off legs, so for carrying two pairs of pants, I get two pairs of long pants and two pairs of shorts. Maybe take one additional, heavier pair of pants for cold or wet weather. But because you have long underwear with you as an underlayer, even the lightweight pants can give you good protection.

Shirts

I pack two or three short-sleeve shirts or T-shirts, one light long-sleeve shirt, and one heavy long-sleeve shirt for colder weather.

Jacket

Pack one good fleece-type jacket or pullover with a hood. If the weather turns really cold, you can layer long underwear, the heavy long-sleeve shirt, your jacket, and even your rain gear jacket.

Rain gear

Good rain gear is an essential item. If you are lucky, you will not need to use the rain gear at all; but when you need the rain gear, good quality is a trip-saver! The tiny, foldable ponchos you buy in the souvenir store are crap for a hike. The very thick plastic things you buy at Walmart will definitely keep water out, but they are totally unbreathable—you will end up sweating to death in forty-degree weather. You will get so wet from the trapped heat and sweat that you might as well not have rain gear at all. Buy a good two-piece rain gear set (with a separate jacket and pants). That way, you can use the jacket for layering or wind protection, as needed.

Baseball cap/hat

Sun protection is important at high altitudes. Plus, you need to cover up your nasty hair. Get a hat with flaps that also can cover your ears and the back of your neck; they are great for discouraging bugs, wind, and cold. I also carry one of those nearly weightless, head-sock things that can cover and warm my entire head, face, and neck for late evenings and cold mornings. I look like a ridiculous criminal, but I am warm and comfortable. It's great for stargazing nights.

There are many good brands of outdoor clothing available, but I have to give a personal shout out to KÜHL. I have found their clothing to be exceptionally durable, comfortable, and efficient on the trail. My KÜHL staples were perhaps a bit pricey up front, but they have lasted well and worked well for years.

Splurge Items

Again, pack weight is an every-step-of-every day issue, so be very choosy about the splurge items you take on a backpacking trip.

Sealock enjoys fly-fishing, so most of his splurge equipment relates to that activity. I enjoy fishing but usually not enough to buy a license and to carry the weight of the extra gear. When I do fish, I carry a cheap, miniature, children's fishing setup from Walmart or Bass Pro. Cool fly-fisherpeople scoff at my uncouth approach, but I still catch and eat fish.

Maybe your splurge item is an electronic device (but please still carry a paper map), or gear for photography, or bird watching or fancy trail cooking. I never carry technology things; the world of technology is a part of what I am trying to escape. Whatever your preferences are, limit yourself to a couple of extraneous items, or you will quickly regret lugging all that dead weight with every step you take.

One of my splurge items has become a staple: a backpacking hammock. Sitting or lying down on something that is not a log or a rock or the ground is a glamorous treat in the wilderness. Eagles Nest Outfitters (ENO) makes fabulous, lightweight, one- or two-person hammocks for backpacking. The strap set weighs more than the hammock does, but it is well worthwhile, both for convenience and for not harming trees. I never go backpacking without one. My other splurge item is a small flask of good, single-malt scotch—a tin cupful is a nice, warm ending to a beautiful day. Any other splurge item will always relate to the particular characteristics of the place I am visiting. Do I need fishing stuff, geology stuff, stargazing stuff, or what?

Food on the Trail

Planning for the food items you will carry is a matter of personal preference. However, keep in mind the following tips:

- Look for high-energy, calorie-heavy, and protein-stocked foods. You are going to be walking hard, and you will need to consume more (good) calories than usual.
- Pack lots of snacks that are easy to consume throughout the day—protein bars, energy bars, nuts, dried fruit, etc.
- Repackage items that come in bulky wrappers. You do not need to carry the extra weight or the leftover trash.
- Do not short yourself on food. Generally, I carry enough food for an extra day.

Some people are trail chefs and get rather complicated with food and prep items. Elaborate meals and food preparations are their splurge items. Not me. I am a very good cook in the comfort of my home, but on the trail, I do not want to spend hours concocting a meal. Give me something easy and quick to prepare, filling, somewhat nutritious, and reasonably edible, and I am good to go. I am hungry; I need fuel; and I want to eat with as little effort as possible.

For lightweight, quick, filling, nutritious, and fairly tasty dinners that you can prepare with your small gas stove in a driving rainstorm, the freeze-dried backpacker meals are impossible to beat. There are tons of culinary choices in any outfitting store. I highly recommend the chili mac. The packages say they contain two servings; I usually eat a whole package by myself. Your appetite may be different. If you are cooking for a group, then "cook" (put a measured amount of boiled water right into the package, stir well, and let it sit for the prescribed number of minutes) two packages for three people. **Understand that you are going to eat every bit of whatever you cook.** There is no garbage disposal on the trail. In fact, someone in your party should be the designated food disposal, eating up anything leftover. Dumping uneaten food invites bears, various rodents, bugs, birds, and all manner of unwanted guests to your campsite. Literally, you should lick everything you use clean, then wash it, then stow it away. Be sure to hang all the trash, food, utensils, and cookware.

On one trip in Colorado, I was starving after a long day on the trail. So, as soon as we made camp, I prepared and ate an entire package of chili mac (enough calories for two people). Meanwhile, Beth spent several hours cooking up some hoagie thing with all kinds of fresh ingredients from a recipe her trail-pro daughter had suggested. She proudly made enough food for five people or so. Mike and I were the only other people there. I was already burping up an extra healthy helping of chili mac. What to do? You can't just leave food lying around. And Beth had worked hard to surprise us. Uncomfortably, but smiling with as much gratefulness as I could muster, I ate enough food for about four hungry people that evening.

Years ago, backpackers had to purchase almost all trail food at outfitting stores. Now, your local grocery store carries a multitude of food items that will work on the trail. You can make and package your own snacks (such as granola, nuts, dried fruit, and chocolate). The light foil (not heavy canned) packages of tuna or chicken or spam are great for lunches. There is an entire aisle of power and protein and energy bars. Instant oatmeal is great for breakfast (but you don't need the cardboard box), especially if you managed to pick some fresh huckleberries along the trail. My local Kroger carries precooked bacon that somehow does not require refrigeration; that stuff cannot possibly be good for you, but damn, bacon tastes good in the morning. Instant coffee crystals, tea bags, sugar packets, packets of peanut butter, and summer sausages requiring no refrigeration can be found in almost any supermarket. You can cook canned biscuits in the coals of a fire with the bit of aluminum foil you carried. Anything you can cook by boiling water will work. For example, get a package of chicken noodle soup mix, boil some water, and add a foil package or two of chicken meat.

Please understand that for me, food is fuel. I simply need fuel for the day and not much more. Your tastes and requirements may be different. With that in mind, here's the way I plan meals for a backpacking trip:

1. Breakfasts

- individual packets of instant coffee and/or teabags and sugar
- two packets of instant oatmeal for each day
- fresh fruit, dried fruit, or granola to add to oatmeal
- precooked bacon or spam or summer sausage or some kind of meat protein to start the day

2. Lunches

- a summer sausage, a lightweight foil package of tuna or chicken or, if I want to splurge, a tin of smoked oysters
- crackers that I repackage into a tin—an old Christmas thing that also serves as an easily accessible lunchbox
- power bars, protein bars, chocolate bars, dried fruits, and nuts to augment lunch throughout the day

3. Dinners

- freeze-dried backpacker meal such as chili mac, sweet and sour pork, or beef stroganoff—easy, quick, and filling and there's little mess or trash
- caffeine-free teabags
- "cup of soup" packages for an appetizer or a warm, late-night snack

4. Day hikes

- for day hikes in the middle of a longer backpacking trip, food means lunch (above) plus some snack bars and nuts
- for day hikes that start in and return to civilization, a fun picnic of fresh fruits, bread, and anything else that will not spoil within one warm day

Weather and Health

When you are outside for the entire duration of your adventure, weather makes all the difference in world. You should regularly reevaluate and constantly adapt to weather conditions on your day hike or backpacking trip. Predictions are helpful, and planning is essential, but weather tends to do its own thing apart from those forecasts and plans—often rapidly and unexpectedly.

Being prepared for a wide variety of possible weather conditions is critical for your safety and well-being—in addition to your comfort level. Many people think very little about the clothing they wear on a day hike. That is a big mistake which can lead to all kinds of other problems. Forget about fashionable tight fits, fabrics that do not breathe well, and matching outfits. Function is everything on the trail.

Many summertime hikers seem to think only of not getting "too hot." They merrily head up the trail in sneakers (with no socks) or sandals, and in short shorts and a cut off T-shirt. But that mountaintop destination is likely to be thirty degrees cooler and windy, with an afternoon rain possible. Be better prepared so you can have a fun day. If you are carrying all of the clothes you might need for four days on a backpacking outing, then you have to plan quite carefully and strategically for a wide variety of conditions.

In warmer temperatures, wear light-colored, loose-fitting, breathable-fabric clothing. Shorts and short-sleeve shirts may be fine, but most often I wear loose-fitting long-sleeve shirts and long pants even in hot weather to keep mosquitos, poison ivy, and whatever else off me and to protect me against sunburn. Wear a hat to shade your head and face.

Be watchful of evolving weather conditions as well as the physical condition of your trail companions. Evaluate those conditions regularly. Do not count on being lucky or just muddling through. Change your plan or turn back if you need to.

Hydration

Dehydration is the number one problem I see on the trail. As I will mention several times in this book, *carry plenty of water and have the ability (a water purifying apparatus and reliable water sources along the trail) to replenish your stock of drinkable water.* During strenuous activity in warm weather, a person should drink two to four cups (four cups is a quart or thirty-two fluid ounces) per hour. Take breaks often and drink often. Do not wait until you are "thirsty"; stay ahead of the hydration curve. Fill up all of your water bottles at every opportunity (unless you know you are following an accessible water source for the entire trail). Understand that caffeine and alcohol *diminish* hydration. What you need is plain water. You might add a powdered sports drink mix to your water to replenish electrolytes.

If you are not urinating as often as you would on any ordinary day, then you are clearly not processing enough water. Hydrate well before you get on the trail, in the mornings and evenings while in camp, and while you are on the trail. Dehydration is problematic and dangerous on its own, and can quickly precipitate much more alarming conditions such as heat exhaustion or heatstroke.

Heat Exhaustion

If the weather is warm and you are doing a strenuous, physical activity, stay well hydrated and be aware of the signs of heat exhaustion. Having the common sense to take plenty of breaks (in the shade if possible) and to drink plenty of water would seem to suffice, but many people get in trouble with heat exhaustion.

Heat exhaustion occurs when people are not properly hydrated and are under physical stress. Note that children produce more body heat and sweat less than adults do. Their reduced ability to get rid of body heat more quickly leads to dehydration and heat exhaustion. Anyone can suffer heat exhaustion, but heavy people are more prone to do so. Typical symptoms are profusely heavy sweating, fatigue, weakness, headache, clammy skin, a weak and rapid pulse, and increased irritability. Body temperature may be elevated (but below 104). Nausea and vomiting are worsening signs. If you show these signs, stop! Find some shade. Loosen your clothing. Drink water. Rest until symptoms dissipate. Drink more water.

Heatstroke

Heatstroke is the dangerous result of unabated dehydration and heat exhaustion. The body loses its ability to shed heat, creating a fever of 105 or more (those high temperatures affect the brain and internal organs). Flushed and dry skin with no sweating and a rapid and strong pulse are emergency warning symptoms. Heatstroke can cause seizures, unresponsiveness, loss of consciousness, and death. You are not prepared to deal with heatstroke in the backcountry. Prevent this chain of events by making sure that you

1. stay well hydrated;
2. take cool-down rest breaks often; and
3. watch for and respond to the signs of heat exhaustion.

The scorching sun, oppressive heat, and lack of water in desert and semidesert environments are quite dangerous. Do not wander into such areas without specific plans for water provisions (likely including the planning of water caching) and for dealing with extreme temperatures. I would strongly suggest that such conditions are for carefully planned and provisioned, partial day hikes—not for long day journeys or for backpacking by recreational hikers.

Cool Weather Concerns

The second-most common problem I see on the trail is lack of preparation for the weather to turn colder (and perhaps wet). Mountainous regions in the United States can hold onto snow well into June—and some places never let go of the snow. Even in midsummer, the temperature at night or in the early morning can drop below freezing. Weather systems can move and change rapidly, quickly dropping the temperature twenty degrees on what seemed like a beautiful, warm summer day. Rain/wetness dramatically increases the cold's effect on your body. Wind and altitude significantly change the temperature's effect too. Even if you start out in your shorts and T-shirt, be prepared to layer on some clothing for warmth and always take rain gear to keep yourself dry. I carry long pants, a long-sleeve shirt, a fleece pullover (preferably with a hood) or a sweater, and rain gear (jacket and pants) with me. Have something with a hood or wear a hat with earflaps (ear and neck-flap hats are also great to keep mosquitos at bay and to avoid sunburn). Body heat is most quickly lost through your head and extremities.

Altitude

The temperature drops 3.3 degrees Fahrenheit for every thousand feet of elevation gain. So, if you work your way up five thousand feet for that mountaintop view, then the temperature dropped 17 degrees with no other factors involved. Your pleasant 70-degree day is now a chilly 53.

Wind Chill

The wind chill factor also comes into play at high elevations. Winds are often much stronger at mountaintops and along passes. A thirty-mile-an-hour wind drops the effective temperature by about ten degrees. So now your pleasant, seventy-degree day has dropped to a cold, windy forty-three on that mountaintop. If you are unprepared, then you are ready to get hypothermia. If one of those common afternoon mountain rains moves in, eliminating the sunshine, dropping the temperature even further, and soaking you, then you are going to be miserable at the least and quite possibly in trouble.

Hypothermia

Hypothermia is a rather commonly occurring condition. Hypothermia happens when your body loses heat faster than it can produce heat. As a result, the core body temperature drops below ninety-six, causing a myriad of reactions and symptoms. Shivering, the body's automatic defense against cold, is usually the earliest and the most noticeable sign. Faster breathing, increased heart rate, lack of coordination, trouble speaking, and slight confusion are also signs of mild to moderate hypothermia. Signs that the condition is worsening include clumsiness, slurred speech, mumbling, drowsiness, trouble thinking clearly, poor decision making, a weak pulse, slow and shallow breathing, and an odd lack of concern about the condition. People often do not recognize hypothermic conditions in themselves; someone else has to take charge. (This is yet another reason not to hike or backpack alone.)

Most people imagine that conditions have to be very cold to bring on hypothermia, but the condition can occur in temperatures as warm as sixty degrees. Being outside for a long time and being fatigued increase the risk of hypothermia. Being wet dramatically increases the chances for hypothermia. Stop and act when you see signs of hypothermia. Get out of the water, rain, and wind if possible. If the affected person is wet and dry clothes are available, then help him or her change into dry, warm clothes immediately. If a sleeping bag is at hand, then get the person into dry clothes and into the bag to warm up. Hot food and warm drinks will help. If symptoms persist or worsen, use your own body heat to warm the affected person—yes, lie down and spoon or embrace him or her, covering yourselves with blankets or jackets or a sleeping bag or whatever you have. Encouraging the person to run or jump around, or rubbing the person to warm him or her up will only worsen the situation. If you catch it early and take prompt action, mild hypothermia usually dissipates relatively soon without ill effects. Ignored and left to worsen, hypothermia can cause loss of consciousness and death.

Hypothermia can easily happen to anyone. A few days into a backpacking trip in New Mexico, Sealock and I took a day hike from base camp to a mountaintop lake. The day was cool but not cold. We did gain three or four thousand feet of altitude. The weather turned cloudy and misty; there was no rain or storm, but a there was a persistent wind and enough mist to make us feel wet. We explored the lake and watched some mountain goats. I walked away to find an appropriate place to dig a hole and do my business. When I got back, Mike said, "We need to head back down or something. I don't feel quite right."

I noticed that he was shivering. I guided him over to the side of a rocky outcrop that offered some protection from the wind and a place to sit. His coordination was just a little bit off. The shirt under his jacket was wet, from either sweat or the mist. Digging into both of our day packs, I found his extra shirt and my extra pullover and got him to change into those clothes. I loaned him my jacket too. The shivers got a little better. We had nothing to make hot drinks or warm food with, but lukewarm water and energy bars are good too. I made him eat and drink some.

"OK, Mike," I said. "You've gotten hypothermic, and we have done just about everything we can do with what we have right here. If we can't get those shivers to stop, then I am going to have to spoon you."

Now quite fully alert, Sealock miraculously claimed to be feeling much, much better. In fact, he thought he was ready to head on back down to camp. Laughing, I told him to sit awhile and to eat and drink more. The shivering soon stopped and, other than Mike being a little tired, all was well. He gave me my jacket back before I got cold, and we hiked four miles or so down to our base camp with no further incident.

Cold Weather Concerns

Some people do winter hiking or backpacking, and I suppose they enjoy it. The stakes are high in this endeavor; make one of a few hundred mistakes, and you could easily die badly. All kinds of specialized equipment may be required: snowshoes, skis, or ice crampons, winter clothing, different tents and sleeping bags, probing tools, avalanche beacons, etc. All kinds of specialized skills are needed, too. For example, one must have excellent wilderness navigation skills and dead-reckoning ability, since any network of trails would be unrecognizable when buried under snow. If you think that a thunderstorm and a day of rain is a bummer during your summer trip, imagine the challenge that a blizzard leaving four feet of snow would be. Most wilderness winter hiking—and all winter backpacking—is out of my league. Back to the first rule: I want to enjoy my trip. If I wanted to discover the wonder of winter-weather wilderness, then I would hire a good, experienced guide who could outfit me, take care of me, and teach me something about how to survive in winter wilderness.

Altitude Sickness

Because atmospheric pressure decreases as you gain altitude, the air you breathe literally thins—becomes less dense—meaning that you neither take in nor absorb as much oxygen with each breath. Getting less oxygen from each breath, the body attempts to compensate by breathing faster and shallower. People who are accustomed to the richer oxygen levels at lower altitudes find it hard to fully "catch their breath" when they visit the mountains—especially when they physically exert themselves. Some people are more or less affected by altitude changes, and no one really knows why. Fitness level plays no role.

Practically everyone will notice some difficulty in adjusting to higher altitude breathing. I notice a very low-grade headache (and a hum in my head) for the first couple of days at altitude. I rarely sleep well the first night at altitude, but after the first night, I am generally so tired that sleep wins anyway. Though I would not try to run a hundred-yard dash, I rarely struggle to catch my breath while hiking, mostly because I have some practice at noticing my breathing patterns and intentionally directing myself to breathe more slowly and more deeply.

Some people, for whatever reason, experience the much more debilitating symptoms of altitude sickness—headache, weakness, tiredness, dizziness, loss of appetite, nausea, confusion, an inability to walk straight, feeling faint, and developing blue or gray lips and fingernails. The only real cure is to go down in altitude at least fifteen hundred feet.

Every person will have some minor troubles adjusting to altitude. But if symptoms are more significant than minor annoyances, then pay attention and respond. Rest. Drink plenty of water. Do not climb to higher altitudes until symptoms dissipate. Give your body some time to adjust to where you are. If symptoms worsen or do not lessen, then get to a lower altitude.

Lightning

Walking along most backcountry trails in areas prone to forest fires, you will see clear signs of lightning strikes in individual burned-out or bizarrely dead and charred trees. Lightning in the backcountry is a big deal; more people die from lightning strikes than from bear and other animal encounters combined.

Be especially careful if you are hiking to bald mountaintops above tree line. Afternoon thunderstorms are common in the mountains in the summer. Plan to start early, have lunch on the mountaintop around noon, and then get off the peak. If thunderstorms appear likely, then do not go to bare, elevated areas.

Clouds with dark underbellies, changing winds and temperatures, and the distinctive scent of rain are all signs of possible storm systems. Do not wait until a thunderstorm engulfs you; make decisions and take action when you see weather threatening. If you can hear thunder, then you need to be concerned about lightning.

The basic principle is to make yourself a less likely lightning rod. Leave open fields, elevated mountaintops, and watery areas. Do not take shelter beneath a solitary tree. Get into a forested area, preferably near a group of smaller trees surrounded by taller trees. Your tent may protect you from rain and wind, but your tent is not a lightning shelter. Designated campsites are generally in forested areas to help protect you from lightning.

If you are caught in an open area, look for a low-lying depression or ravine. Become the shortest and smallest target possible. Crouch with your head between your knees. Do not lie down flat on the ground—you actually want to minimize your contact with the ground.

People who have survived direct strikes or near strikes often describe a prestrike moment in which their bodies respond to the strong electric field with positive streamers. They describe a sensation of tingling and/or hair standing on end. If you are near a thunderstorm and experience these sensations, then you are in immediate danger of a close-proximity lightning strike. Crouch quickly and tuck your head. Hold your breath to avoid breathing in the superheated air surrounding a lightning bolt. You might also want to pray.

Rain

With luck, occasional rain is just a minor inconvenience on your trip. Good-quality, somewhat-breathable rain gear (a jacket with a hood and pants) is essential for any backpacking trip. Most trails become water channels during any lasting rain. Rock becomes slick, and dirt becomes mud; you have to move more slowly and carefully in rain to avoid falls. Do not attempt to cross flood-swollen, fast-moving rivers or creeks. You may have to burn a day mostly in your tent or under a tarp waiting for a rain system to pass. Chill out and play cards or something. Wet weather means colder and possibly windier conditions, so stay as dry as possible and layer your clothing to avoid hypothermia.

Mountainous regions flood quickly with persistent rain. Lots of water moves downward hard and fast. If you are in a designated campsite in a national park, most likely the spot is not prone to flashflooding. If you pick your own campsite in a less-regulated area (a state park or even a federal wilderness area), then avoid canyons, ravines, or anything else with steep walls to trap and channel water. Avoid low-lying areas adjacent to rivers and streams. Get to—and stay on—higher ground.

Canyon land areas and arid environments flashflood extremely quickly and with catastrophic consequences. Slot canyons and dry riverbeds are deathtraps during rain events. Never explore such areas without having the highest confidence in a dry forecast for your location and upstream of your location. Get out ASAP at any sign of rain.

Flashflooding is a serious danger. The local river I often explore for fossils has high, steep walls that are practically impossible to climb when dry and ready to create landslides when wet. Places to get down into or to climb out of the river can be miles apart. Generally, there is barely a foot of water in that river; but a good rain turns it into a thirty-foot-deep torrent that can tear out the walls that hem it in and carry all manner of rocks, trees, and debris. Those powerful waters are great for churning up fossils, but they would be fatal to a person caught in the flood. Even a really cool fossil is not worth your life. Effectively, twenty miles of that river is a slot canyon.

Snow

Snow may linger year-round at high elevations. In the lower forty-eight, snow can fall at high elevations in almost any month, though it's rare in July and even rarer in August. Although you may live in an area that experiences a long, pleasant fall, wintery weather comes early (in late September) and lingers (into May and even June) in the mountains. Many of the roads, trails, and facilities at our most famous national parks close at the end of September and may not be fully open or passable until late June or early July.

The problems with encountering a snowpack on the trail are all the things you cannot tell by looking at the snow. How deep is it? Is there a hole, or maybe a ravine, hiding underneath there? How about rocks, spikey dead trees, or water? Is the snowpack stable? (Likely not; the whole thing is melting.) It is thin or thick? You just can't tell for certain. If the trail you are on has a clear, well-worn (and recently worn) path through the snowpack, then proceed with caution. If there is no clear path, then skirt the edges to get around a snowpack and return to the trail. Proceed slowly. Use a walking stick to check for holes and depth.

Hiking to the summit of Mount Holmes in Yellowstone one July, Sealock and I encountered several large snowpacks obliterating the trail. Not only did we have the problem of figuring a way around the snowpack, we also had to find the trail again. There was no discernable path, nor were there footsteps in front of us. We stopped and evaluated. We made sure we spotted places well above us where the trail emerged again. We discussed several routes through the pack, which mostly skirted the edges of the snow and then put us back on the trail. We made a good plan, proceeded cautiously, and enjoyed the rest of the hike. Another time, in Glacier National Park, we had to turn back on a hike because the snowpack was just too big and there were too many unknowns to formulate a good plan.

Ice

Ice is really no good at all. Never trust ice. You can easily slip, fall, or fall through. Just avoid ice—unless you have the experience (or a guide) and the equipment to deal with it. Never put ice in a good single-malt scotch, either.

Tides

Some wonderful wilderness places, like Olympic National Park, have beautiful and wild beach trails along craggy ocean shores. Sounds like fun, right? Those trails are fun and quite safe—*as long as you have a tide chart and you pay strict attention to it*. At some points during the day, you can walk right down the beach. At other points during the day, you would be pummeled against the rocks and dragged out to sea if you stood in that same spot. Know where you are, know the forces at work, and plan well to be in the right spots at the right times.

Wildfires

Wildfires are a common natural (and sometimes human-induced) phenomenon in wilderness areas. How do you survive a wildfire? You really do not want to put yourself in that situation. Wildfires are fast and unpredictable. Trained, experienced, well-equipped, professional firefighters die every year trying to control these rampaging beasts. Stay well clear of areas experiencing wildfires. A national park such as Yellowstone is a very big place, so you can still enjoy the park while some areas within the park are experiencing wildfires. Heed warnings and signs. (Remember; don't be stupid.) Evacuate when you are warned to. If you are not in a national park, consult the appropriate websites or check with the closest ranger station or forest service station. Ask about conditions and active fires in the area before you go in. Change your plans if wildfires are running near an area you hoped to visit. The very best advice concerning wildfires is to stay clear of them.

If you are somehow surprised by a wildfire (which is highly unlikely these days), then clear out. Breathe through a bandanna or another item of clothing. Heat and embers rise, so you want to get below a fire, if possible. You are not going to outrun a fire by climbing up. However, if you are already near the top of a ridge with a fire below you, then scramble the ridge and go down the other side. Try to get to lower, large, level spaces with no combustible material—a lake, a river, or an already burned-out area. Stay out of canyons or chutes if you are making your way down through a fire; they act like funnels for heat moving upward.

Please, please, please do not contribute to starting wildfires. Nature makes plenty of these destructive events all by itself. If there is a burn ban and/or a high fire-danger warning in the area you are visiting, then do not make fire. If conditions are good and you are permitted to make a fire, do so in a proper fire pit—and make damn sure your fire is out and your coals are dead before you leave.

What If the Supervolcano Beneath Yellowstone Explodes?

Well, good luck to us all.

Getting There: Airplanes and Travel

Backpacking trips, for me, usually mean traveling a long distance. Because vacation time is short and nights in the wilderness are precious, an airline flight is usually the first leg. With current Transportation Security Administration (TSA) rules, flying your gear requires some special planning.

Some items critical to your backpacking trip are not allowed on a plane either in carry-on or checked baggage, namely, stove fuel, fire starters, matches, and bear spray. Essentially, anything combustible or containing highly compressed air is a no-no. Your first planning step is *not* putting any of those things in your checked bag. You are packing all kinds of unusual gear and tools for this trip, so your checked bag will undoubtedly set off every alarm and search parameter the TSA has. Since 9/11, I have never gone on a backpacking trip without finding my stuff rearranged and one of those notes from the TSA about searching my checked bag. If you try to smuggle your stove gas in, you likely will land without the bag containing all of your gear.

Do not attempt to check a backpack as luggage or all sorts of gear and attachments will go missing. Buy one of those giant cargo bags from REI or Eagle Creek and zip your backpack (and everything else you can fit) into it.

Because you cannot carry some necessary items on the plane, you will need to plan your trip schedule so that you can purchase airline-banned items such as bear spray, stove fuel, and matches after you land. Do some Internet research and know where you can find an appropriate store—and when the store is open for business—before you leave home. Landing midday or early afternoon is always the best option. Airports are generally not adjacent to national parks or wilderness areas, so you probably have some driving to do. Get your rental car, find the extra provisions you need, get a hotel room or car campsite near your put-in point, and stay the night. Scout out the area, have a nice dinner, and generally enjoy yourself before you hit the trail in the morning. This schedule allows you a leisurely evening in which you can lay out all of the stuff for your backpacking trip, check your list one more time, pare down weight one more time, and then organize your pack correctly so you are ready to hit the trail.

Before you board a plane to go home, remember to take all of those banned substances out of your pack again. I always look for a Boy Scout troop, a newly arrived backpacker, or a park ranger to give my leftover stove fuel and bear spray to. In all of my years of backpacking, I have never actually had to fire a canister of bear spray. The stuff is not cheap, and everyone in the group has an unused canister left when we come off the trail. Pass it on. I have given away many perfectly good cans of bear spray. To date, I have yet to be the recipient of one.

Before 9/11, none of these airline rules was an issue. No one seemed to care what you took on a plane. I remember coming home from a trip in the Pecos Wilderness in New Mexico in the mid-1990s. I was catching a flight out of Albuquerque the same evening we got off the trail. (Bad plan. Get a hotel room or campsite for the night you get off the trail. Take a long shower, enjoy a big meal and some scotch, and then fly out the next day. Much less stressful.) A dutifully planned stopped at a Kampground of America (KOA) to buy a shower on my way to the airport did not work out; the water was out of service. No shower. I had not bathed in five days. Oh well, on to the airport—I had to catch a flight. I boarded a flight with no assigned seating. I am sure I had stove gas and several flammable materials in my checked luggage. On my person, I had a large, folding hunting knife. I was also carrying a four-foot-tall, pine walking stick adorned with an elk vertebra on the crown and bejeweled with feathers and small quartz stones. Several bear teeth were hanging from it on a wire. All of these things, including the stick, I had found along the trail. Besides wearing the cleanest clothes I had left (which had had maybe two days of wear), I had also wrapped a tie-dyed bandanna around my head as a do-rag. Another bandanna, wrapped around my left hand and secured with some duct tape, was covering and protecting an accidental cut. I found a seat by a window, propped my bear-toothed shaman stick against it, pulled out the tray in front of me, got out my knife, and started cutting up an apple for a snack. For a while, no one chose the two seats next to me. As the plane filled up, a woman and her daughter, who was eight or so, came down the aisle looking for seats. Two seats were available beside me. Being a friendly person who is actually quite good with children, as I saw the girl draw nearer, I smiled and offered her a piece of apple. She screamed and sat down in the aisle. In between wails, she told her mother that she did not want to sit beside the "scary man." Kids.

As a sidenote, I just looked over my shoulder to see that bear-toothed walking stick I made on the trail more than twenty years ago sitting in the corner of my office. Memories from the trail last a lifetime.

If you have the time, you might want to drive to your destination in an epic road trip. Sealock and I have done this a couple of times. Texas is a very long way from anywhere topographically interesting; so, once, we got a cheap flight to Denver and then drove up into the northeastern corner of Wyoming for some dinosaur hunting on a remote ranch. We imagined that there would be all kinds of interesting scenery along the way. We were wrong. We drove for hours and hours and hours through High Plains grasslands. It was like being in an ocean of tall grass with no other land in sight despite the incredibly vast horizon. Apparently, the wind blew constantly (and hard) from the west most of the year, because the several dozen trees we saw in eight hours were mangled and bent eastward at a forty-degree angle. Tall, angled snow fences (to keep blowing, drifting snow from swamping the interstate or highway) went on for miles and miles and miles. We theorized that being in the fencing business might be the only way to make a living in this part of the country. When we finally found an exit with services, we stopped at a diner and quizzed the server about how the winters were. Mike and I are always trying to get into and to explore these more remote places; but the local people we meet – especially young people – seem mostly interested in trying to get out of these kinds of areas. We theorized that when people finally found the courage to leave these places, they would drive for six hours or so seeing absolutely nothing, which would convince them that there was really nothing else in the world to get to, and they would simply return home.

Road trips take a lot of extra time, but they can be great for several reasons. First, you can throw all of your stuff in a car and organize it later. No need to worry about airline regulations. Secondly, you can adjust your trip schedule to whatever looks interesting at a moment's notice. On a different trip—this time to South Dakota—Sealock and I saw the giant presidents' heads carved into Mount Rushmore, dropped by biker-famous Sturgis, went to Deadwood and found his grandfather's grave near Calamity Jane's, stopped by the really cool Mammoth Dig (which has turned up other Pliocene Epoch animals as well) in Hot Springs, and drove to Devil's Tower (a stunning natural attraction in the middle of nowhere) in a wandering route to our remote ranch fossil-hunting destination.

The drive back to Denver from northeastern Wyoming was just as long as the drive out had been. We had stayed in Casper, Wyoming, a town with an awful hotel nearest the ranch on which we were dinosaur hunting. The ranch was sixty miles from the town on a mostly dirt (or worse) road. We got a financial deal if we provided a car for the group trip; so, of course, we provided our rental car, which I got to use on free days. After four days of transporting people through unbelievably sticky Cretaceous mud to and from the ranch, we left for Denver one night. On the way out of town, we stopped at a car wash and spent about forty dollars in quarters trying to wash that Cretaceous mud off the undercarriage of the rental car. There was still so much mud underneath the car that it shook violently if we went over fifty miles an hour. That problem likely saved our lives, however. On the eight-hour drive back to Cheyenne, Wyoming, we saw a sign every few miles warning about deer crossings. Even traveling at fifty miles per hour, we barely avoided collisions with several dozen deer. Road trips are awesomely epic and memorable...if you have the time.

Dark Sky

f you live near any kind of city, nothing will prepare you for the sheer astonishment of stargazing on a dark, cloudless (and cold) night in the wilderness. In most populated areas of the country, light pollution blurs people's view of the stars. Because we have conquered the dark with man-made light, the night sky glows (actually "fogs") hundreds of times brighter than natural starlight conditions—even a hundred miles from urban development. If you are a city-dweller, like the majority of the population, then you might routinely see a few planets or the brightest star clusters. Perhaps you can pick out one of the dippers or recognize the constellation Orion on a particularly clear winter night. But you have no idea how many beautiful points of light are out there when nightfall brings an actually dark sky. There are so many points of light in a truly dark sky that identifying constellations is nearly impossible. You would not believe how bright the moon is when it's high and full; you can literally read by moonlight.

The Bortle scale, ranging from one to nine, measures dark sky conditions by phenomena observable to the naked eye. Inner-city conditions are a nine on the scale: the moon and a planet or two may be visible, but not much else. Far-flung suburbs might be rated a five: clouds are still noticeably lit from below, finding any constellation will be difficult, and the beautiful spill of our own Milky Way Galaxy is an indistinguishable smudge.

Get to a remote wilderness area that might be a one or a two on the Bortle scale, and you will think that you are standing on another planet and staring into a universe that you never imagined existed. In fact, that universe has been there all along, waiting for you to discover it through the recent veil of civilization. You are seeing the night sky as our ancestors did *every night* for thousands of years. You will understand why every culture on the planet was fascinated by the night sky—basing calendars on it and finding among the stars pictures and gods and the stuff of stories. In the last hundred years, most people on the planet have lost—and completely forgotten about—this basic human experience of wondering about the vast night sky.

Not only will you see the intricate structure of our home Milky Way Galaxy arcing across the sky, you may notice that some regions cast a noticeable dark shadow. Clouds are now only visible as dark holes against the sky. There are so many points of light that you will struggle to identify common constellations. Nearly all of those light points are entire distant galaxies—structures of billions of stars—and not a single shining star at all. You may see the yellow-to-orange color of the zodiacal light, a ghostly glow from our star, the sun, hidden behind the turning Earth. You can pick out the reflected light of our multitude of tiny satellites racing across the sky. Shooting stars—small meteors burning upon entry to our atmosphere—occasionally flash and disappear. Looking through an ordinary pair of binoculars, you will think you got your hands on the Hubble Telescope. If you happen to be camping at a quiet lake, you will see stars shimmering on the still water as if the sky were both above and below you (which is true). There is nothing more beautiful, humbling, and thought provoking than finally seeing the wonder and mystery of the cosmos with your own eyes.

Because of weather or vantage points, I don't always get a good stargazing night, but that experience is always a goal. A good stargazing night is the highlight of any backpacking trip. Bundle up; nights are usually cold. Find an open vantage point. Lie on the ground. Be still. Look long. Breathe deeply. Make up your own constellations and stories, or just let your mind wander. Look longer. Breathe deeper. Enjoy. And if you wake up in the wee hours of any dark morning to relieve yourself, plan to stay out for a little while, looking up at the sky. You will be glad you did. In fact, you may decide that you love backpacking just so you can see a dark sky from time to time.

On one trip in New Mexico, we spent hours gazing at stars, pointing at falling stars, and tracking satellites. We tried to do enough geometry and math in our heads to figure out when a satellite would reappear along the same path. One evening, Lisa and I saw what must have been a distant supernova explosion. If you are in a national park and find some kind of stargazing program on the rangers' schedule, plan to attend. At Badlands National Park, I sat in a small, dark amphitheater with a few people and a knowledgeable ranger, brushing up on constellation identification and then watching the International Space Station fly from horizon to horizon on schedule. In Hawaii, several good telescopes were set up so novices like me could clearly see the beautiful structures and colors of various galaxies and nebulae. The universe is an awesome place.

Even on short trips, being in the backcountry brings a different day and night rhythm. Sunlight will wake you up early in the morning. When night comes, your day is done. You can sit with a cup of tea and talk around a campfire for a while (if a fire is permissible). You can decide to bundle up and do some stargazing nearby, or you can settle into your sleeping bag for the night. Do not wander around looking for something to do at night. It is damn dark. And probably quite cold. There is nothing to do when the dark settles in. And most predatory animals you might be concerned about are nocturnal. Just sleep tight.

One year, Sealock and I intentionally camped and hiked in an area of Yellowstone that had several wolf packs. Our base camp was in a forest on the edge of a broad meadow through which a stream (with tasty trout) ran. The second night in, around midnight, individual wolf howls began as if the pack were gathering or communicating while hunting. It was the coolest thing I have ever heard in my life—a bucket-list moment. Three or four hours later, I woke to the sound of a bunch of wolves going crazy—howling, yipping, barking—relatively close by. We later guessed they had a made a kill. Some kind of party was going on. I will never forget that night. Of course, both Mike and I were quite content to stay in our respective tents and listen without investigating. Commentary could wait until daylight, coffee, and breakfast.

Someday, I will plan a trip that provides a good opportunity to see the northern lights—an experience that I have not yet checked off my personal bucket list.

Water

Something about water—not the kind that falls from the sky to dampen my day—just makes me happy. I want to see lakes, streams, rivers, waterfalls, and pools, although I am not quite so enamored with insect-infested bogs and marshes. I intentionally plan trips with plenty of water features and water access. Seeing a perfectly still lake mirroring mountains and trees and sunset is awesome. The colors in clear, cool waters are amazing. There is nothing more calming than simply listening to a stream. Every waterfall is art in motion. The sea is mesmerizing.

A consistent supply of clean, purified water is also necessary for your physical well-being. During strenuous activity, you may need two quarts of water or more per hour. Staying comfortably hydrated on a backpacking trip, along with cooking and cleaning, could require four or five gallons of water per person per day. Water is extremely heavy. A gallon of fresh water weighs 8.36 pounds. You are not likely to carry five gallons of water (better than forty pounds) in your pack for a day, so you need regular access to dependable water sources along the trail as well as the ability to purify water for drinking, cooking, and cleaning. If need demands, a person can get by with less water for a while—but shorting water for days is a terrible idea.

There are beautiful places in this country that I have not explored because dependable water sources are limited. Remember rule one: enjoy your trip. I do not enjoy carrying forty pounds of water. I do not enjoy being thirsty or testing the limits of hydration. I do not enjoy the extra planning and effort of water caching for an arid trip. Maybe someday I will go for all of the extra planning and effort and precautions necessary to take such a trip. For now, I prefer water in abundance, thank you.

The gorgeous stream or lake you are standing by will look like the purest, cleanest, coolest water you have ever seen, but do not be fooled. Drinking that water, unfiltered or unpurified, puts you at risk for a host of waterborne illnesses. You are not going to die right away, nor will you likely die at all; but you may contract a miserable case of wilderness diarrhea. The incubation period for those problems may be a day or two—or even seven days, so you might pay for your carelessness after you trip is over. Bacteria, viruses, and/or parasites can live happily in those waters. Giardia and Cryptosporidium are somewhat common culprits. Most waterborne illness issues are caused by normal animal activity (drinking, urinating, and defecating in and around water sources), so beware of areas heavily traversed by pack animals. Drinking the water is certainly better than dying of dehydration, so drink if the need is dire. However, the safe solution is simple; always filter and purify your water. Iodine pills work, but there is a significant time delay before you can drink, and the resulting water tastes terrible. UV radiation contraptions work well, but I prefer the tried-and-true hand-pump filters. Such pump filters last a long time, can work if your water source is less than clear, clean easily, and are almost indestructibly reliable. Best of all, you can drink the cold filtered water immediately. No method is perfect, but in thirty years of using hand-pump filters, I have never had a case of wilderness diarrhea. By the way, the most effective means of purifying is to boil the water for a couple of minutes.

Choose water that looks as clean (clear) as possible. Moving water (natural filtering) is best, although water from a lake that is still enough for sediments and bacteria to settle to the bottom is also good. Avoid using water that is stagnant, smelly, discolored, or unclear. If you are wise, then you made camp near a reliable water source. So I don't have to hike down to the water source constantly, I always carry some kind of light, collapsible water bucket or a foldable container that holds a few gallons and can be hung from a tree. Conveniently, we can boil that water to purify or cook, and we can use that water to wash our faces or hands.

Remember that you need purified water not just for drinking, but also for cooking and for cleaning your eating utensils and dishes. Always keep a pot of boiled, hot water near your camp kitchen area. People can use that water for hot drinks and for cleaning their eating utensils.

Water—so beautiful and so necessary for life—has another quality that people often fail to recognize. Water is likely the most dangerous thing you will encounter along the trail. Although there are remarkably few serious accidents and deaths in our national parks, the majority of those incidents have something to do with water. Water makes rock slippery, so falling accidents in and around water are common. The areas above and below waterfalls are especially dangerous. Currents, even in a small river or stream, can be swift—a foot of water can take a person down easily—and cause falls or sweep people into all kinds of hazards. And, of course, you could drown.

Some mountain lakes are stunningly steep and deep. Practically all of these bodies of water are quite cold, exacerbating hypothermic effects. There are exceptions: in Yellowstone, we came across an entire stream off the trail to Bridal Veil Falls that had so much geothermally warmed water pumped into it that the entire stream was a comfortable spa. But be careful! Rawer thermal features (unmixed with many more parts of fresh water) are hot and acidic enough to be deadly, and the ground near them is often thin and unsafe!

Here are my five rules about water:

1. Always carry enough water (at least two thirty-two-ounce containers per person). If you are camping, as opposed to day hiking, also carry a collapsible bucket or water container for camp use.
2. Always have the ability to replenish filtered and purified water.
3. Always plan your trail route and campsites around the reliable availability of water. Drink deeply and replenish your water supplies practically every time you have the opportunity.
4. Always be especially careful and cautious around water.

5. Always wear good water shoes with sturdy soles when wading through or swimming in water to avoid foot injuries and falls.

River crossings

Some wilderness trails include river or stream crossings. Below are some tips for safely wading across rivers:

- Evaluate the crossing. Is the shallowest and best place to cross at the trail? (That is likely so.) Is the water too deep and/or too swift to cross safely? (Moving water that is much above your knees will make the crossing quite difficult.) What hazards, such as fallen trees or logjams, exist? The water you are crossing should be clear. If water is muddy and you cannot see the bottom, then probe for the bottom very carefully and cautiously or do not cross at all.
- Change into your sturdy water shoes, securing your hiking boots and socks in or on your pack. If you do not have water shoes, then cross the river in your hiking boots. Barefooting is never a good idea.
- If some people in your group are less adept at crossing than others are, then you may want to tie one end of a rope on the entrance side of the crossing and send a scout across the river to tie off the other end of the rope. The rope will not do much for people's balance or stability, but it does provide a safety grab/hold if someone falls.
- *Unbuckle your pack* (belt and chest straps) before wading into the river. Let the pack hang loosely from the shoulder straps alone. This way, if you fall, you can quickly slip out of your pack instead of being trapped with a heavy, waterlogged pack that could pull you underwater and sweep you downstream. Again, if the crossing is more challenging for some of your companions (or if you are simply a gentleman), then you may want to have an experienced person cross back and forth several times just to carry packs, so that others can make the crossing unencumbered.

- A walking stick (which simply can be a sturdy stick you just picked up) is a very useful tool in river crossings. Firmly plant the walking stick *downstream* from you and just ahead of you with each step. This gives you have a third point of contact to lean into that greatly aids in balance.

You will frequently cross small streams, runoffs, mudholes, and marshy bogs on many trails. You should be wearing good, mostly waterproof, hiking boots. Just step in the stuff and move on. Your boots are made for that kind of walking. Jumping, hopping, contorting, or otherwise going out of your way to avoid two inches of water or mud is just a good way to accidentally fall. It is not as though you are not going to get dirty on this trip. Just walk right through the stuff.

Fire

Hard to beat sitting around a campfire at night, talking and laughing with friends. Small campfires, when permissible, are fun. There are some rules and best practices to follow, however.

First, make sure that a campfire is permissible in the area where you make camp. National parks, federal wilderness areas, and state parks have different rules at different times, so get current information. Because of the dangers of dry spells and wildfire conditions, such areas frequently institute fire bans. Some areas have permanent fire bans. Usually, there will be clear signs about fire conditions and bans as you drive into the area, but checking with the ranger station or area employees for up-to-date information is always best. Please play by the rules. Do not make fires when or where fires are banned.

Do not make fires anywhere you please. Campfires are for existing campsites. To avoid trampling more and more of the wilderness you are visiting, use an existing campsite and use an existing fire pit/fire ring.

If there is no fire pit at your campsite, then make a proper fire ring before building a fire. Choose a level, open area away from your tents. Clear an area about ten feet in diameter. Dig a shallow pit in the center—about a foot deep. Ring the pit with stones.

Wind makes fire dangerous by transporting small, hot embers to places where they could start additional fires. Do not make a fire in windy conditions.

Burn only already downed wood. Do not burn any trash other than paper. Keep your fire under control; this is a small campfire, not a fraternity bonfire. Do not leave a fire unattended. Allow your wood to burn completely to ash. *Most importantly, put your fire completely out before you leave.*

Here are some tips for putting out a campfire:

- If the fire area is still quite warm, then the embers are not out.
- Pour water on the fire area until all hissing sounds stop.
- If you do not have water, then cover or bury the fire area with sand or dirt.
- After you think you have put out your fire well, check it one more time. Turn over the ashes with a shovel or stir them with a stick to make sure no embers are still smoldering. If the area is still warm or if you uncover hot embers, then pour on more water and/or bury the fire with more dirt.

Always have two reliable ways to make fire (and to light your gas stove). I carry wooden matches and a cheap lighter. While you are out, practice other ways to make fire—glass refraction, flint or various strike-stick methods, or making a bow drill or fire bow. You may never actually need the skills, but the practice is fun.

Mother Nature

You may get caught up in all kinds of emotions while soaking in the beauty and grandeur of nature. I understand and agree. Poets have done the same for millennia. But before you get too cuddly personifying nature as some kindly, mothering goddess, you should understand that nature is oblivious to your adoration. In fact, nature would just as soon see you slaughtered and eaten at the beautiful spot you stand upon. Nature is not your friend. You may love nature, but nature does not especially love you back. Nature is not hanging around to hug you or to feed you or to tuck you in at night. On the contrary, nature has a million ways to kill you and will not miss you when you are gone.

If you want to attach a human feeling to nature, then that feeling should be respect. Learn to respect (and how to adapt to) cold, heat, wind, water, ice, rock, mountains, storms, thermal features, etc. Learn to respect the balance that nature upholds. Having a juvenile crush on nature will get you into all kinds of trouble. Learn, instead, to respect nature.

I sincerely hope that you will decide to love nature and to treat the Earth kindly, but your love will be unrequited. Nature will have no opinion about you. You are one of innumerable species to come and go across nature's Earth-stage over the last four and a half billion years. All of human history amounts to a couple of breaths in the long course of nature. Nature does not subscribe to our fascinatingly comical human tendency to think that everything in the universe revolves around us and exists for our sake. Nature is a much more awesome and enduring thing, always continuing its own course, while we scuttle around about our business.

About Bears (and Other Creatures)

O K, so everybody thinks he or she needs to worry about bears, right? Well, in a national park backcountry, you are much more likely to suffer injuries or death from (in order) a water accident or drowning, a car accident, a fall, a lightning strike, or an encounter with a bison or an elk than you are to be mauled by a bear. You may go backpacking for years without ever seeing a bear, much less getting hurt by one. Bear attacks are, statistically, extremely rare. However, a hiker should still religiously practice the protocols that minimize bear interactions.

On September 16, 2016, wideopencountry.com published an article by Lindi Smith containing data about human deaths caused by animals. She compiled data from each state that revealed the animals most deadly to people. The data is fascinating. A person in the United States is 120 times more likely to die from a deer encounter (mostly car accidents) than from an interaction with a bear, a mountain lion, or a shark. A person is six hundred times more likely to die from a deer encounter than from an incident with a wolf. The deadliest animals in America (in order) are deer (car accidents), bees/wasps/hornets (allergic reactions), and dogs. Cows and horses are tied for the fourth spot, and then we move to spiders. Bears, mountain lions, alligators, and sharks are way down the list, with only one death per year from each one, on average. They are tied with cone snails for deadliness. I do not know what a cone snail is, but I assume that I can manage to outrun one. Snakes are three thousand times less likely to kill you than a deer is. Coyotes are twelve thousand times less likely to kill you than a deer is. So why are we so troubled by bears, mountain lions, sharks, wolves, coyotes, and snakes? In my own phobia world, I instinctively knew that spiders were worse than that lot was.

Back to bears, then. Bears are not particularly interested in you, nor are bears generally looking for opportunities to hunt you. Bears do not like being surprised by your presence, however, and may feel threatened enough to attack in order to protect their young, their territory, or themselves.

Bears are very interested in all of the delicious, odd scents associated with you and your stuff—your food, that candy bar snack, that minty fresh toothpaste, your trash, etc. Bears are omnivores and scavengers, always happy to eat the closest and easiest meal they can get. Wilderness protocols about securing all of your food, scented items, and trash away from your campsite are extremely important safety precautions. Never leave such inviting smells strewn about your base camp or in your tent.

If you are hiking to designated wilderness campsites in a national park, you will likely be required to watch a bear-safety video at the ranger station before you receive your permit. If you have questions, ask the ranger. Within national parks, bear activity is monitored and managed to minimize bears' contact with humans. At the ranger station, you may find that the area you wish to hike or camp in has been closed due to an increase in bear activity; in that case, the rangers will issue a permit to you for a different area or site.

Bears are unpredictable and moody. Park rules (the violation of which are fineable offenses) require people to stay one hundred yards from bears and at least twenty-five yards from other wild animals. If you are fortunate enough to see a bear, first make sure that you are a safe distance away to view the bear. Never, under any circumstances, should you move closer or toward a bear for a better view. Never, under any circumstances, should you ever move toward or closer to that cute cub. In fact, you should be figuring out how to slowly back even farther away until the bear moves off and goes about its business. If you want a close-up picture of a bear (or any other wild animal), then invest in a camera with an excellent, long range, zoom lens.

How do you avoid surprising a bear? If you are hiking with a group of three or more people, talking, and making noise, you are unlikely to surprise a bear. Avoid hiking alone. Avoid hiking very early or late in the day. Do not hike at night. The silly bear bells only annoy people like me. Talk loudly or clap your hands if you need to make noise.

Bears often use the convenient system of wilderness trails. Finding signs of bears, such as bear scat, is common. If you encounter a bear moving in your direction along a trail, slowly back out of the way as far as you can to let the bear pass. Keep the animal's line of travel and escape paths clear. Get your bear spray in hand and be ready to fire.

Do not ever run, no matter what the bear does. Running may trigger the predator/prey response. You are not going to outrun the bear anyway. Back away slowly and deliberately.

If your movement agitates the bear, then stop. Huffing, swaying the head back and forth, clacking teeth, and flattened ears are signs of agitation. A bear may stand on its hind legs to get a better view of you. Try again to back away slowly, but stop if your movement further irritates the bear.

Use your peripheral vision to watch the bear. Avoid making eye contact with the bear. The bear will take a stare as a sign of aggression. Turn sideways to the animal. Do your best to look as nonthreatening and as calm as possible.

Ranger instructions and videos will tell you to talk quietly to the bear. I am not sure why. Maybe you should complement the bear profusely. Say nice things to the bear such as, "My, what big claws you have" to convince the bear that you are friendly. I suspect this advice to talk quietly to the bear is more of a trick to keep you (or me) calm than anything to do with the bear. Continue to back away slowly and deliberately.

If a bear continues toward you—or even charges—*do not run.* Stop. Prepare to fire your bear spray. The majority of bear charges are bluffs, so stand your ground. If the bear gets within ten yards of you, fire the spray several times in two- or three-second bursts, aiming just above the bear's head.

Studies show that bear spray works very effectively. In fact, bear spray is far more effective than firearms are. Two studies of bear encounters by University of Calgary bear expert Steve Herrero showed that 98 percent of people deploying bear spray escaped a bear encounter unharmed (other than probably soiling their pants). In contrast, in bear encounters in which people relied on guns for protection, 56 percent of gun toters were injured or killed, and 61 percent of the bears died. US Fish and Wildlife Service reports also support the effectiveness of bear spray. For an excellent summary of Steve Herrero's research, see Nick Heil's article "Shoot or Spray? The Best Way to Stop a Charging Bear" in the May 7, 2012, edition of *Outside* magazine. I know that gun-crazy America thinks a firearm magically makes people safe and invincible, but real data about bear encounters does not support that belief. Bear spray is much more effective, much lighter to carry, much easier to aim and to fire effectively, and it is much less likely to injure or kill the user in some other accidental firing. Moreover, the disabling effects of bear spray on the animal are not permanent or fatal. Carry a gun around, if that makes you feel better, but you damn sure should have bear spray with you in bear country.

Some people mistakenly think that bear spray is some kind of proactive repellent. There have been reports of people bear-spraying a camping area or their tents or backpacks, as if the smell alone repels bears. The opposite is actually true; the inert pepper smell will attract the attention of bears for a couple of days. Bear spray works at close range (within thirty feet or so), because the cloud of highly concentrated, irritating materials attacks the sensitive membranes of the bear's eyes, nose, and mouth.

If a bear reaches you, fall to the ground to protect your stomach and abdomen while your pack protects your back. Clasp your hands behind your neck. If the bear rolls you over, roll quickly back onto your stomach. The bear is probably not trying to eat you. The bear wants to eliminate you as a threat. There is still a good chance that the bear will stop the attack once it recognizes that you are no longer a threat.

By the way, the dude (who apparently could not be killed no matter what ridiculous things he did) in *The Revenant* pretty much did everything wrong in the movie's gruesome bear-attack scene. He heard a bear and then kept exploring. He saw a bear cub in the wilderness. Instead of immediately backing away from the area, he got curious and kept moving toward the cub. He believed in the magic of his almighty flintlock gun. (I do not remember him talking quietly and kindly to the bear, either.) The mamma bear, protecting her cub, attacked him. Did you notice that the mamma bear stopped the attack after disabling the threat? She ambled away to check on her cub. And what did our hero do? Lie there quietly and play dead? No, he decided that he needed to crawl off to retrieve his magical gun. When the mamma bear saw that the threat was moving again, she attacked again. Viciously.

If a bear visits your campsite at night, get your spray ready and put some shoes on, but otherwise stay quietly in your tent. The bear is much more interested in the food bag you hung well away from your tent, or maybe in some goodies you left in your pack, than it is in you. If you are with a group of people and a bear approaches your campsite, you might try gathering your group together and making a lot of noise to drive away the visitor.

Some people worry a lot about the difference between black bears and grizzly bears. Grizzlies do have a reputation for being more aggressive; but really, a bear is still a bear—all of them are potentially dangerous animals. Color and size are not reliable distinguishing characteristics. Grizzlies have a distinctive hump between their shoulders, rounded ears, and large (up to four inches long) white claws. Black bears (which come in a variety of colors) have no shoulder hump, pointed ears, and smaller, dark claws. If you are close enough to a bear to notice the exact size and color of its claws, then you are in grave danger.

One of my favorite Facebook memes purportedly is a picture of a sign from Fort Steele Campground in British Columbia. Of course, who knows if anything on social media is actually true. But I still laughed at the sign meme, which read:

We advise the outdoorsman to wear noisy little bells on cloth-
ing so as to give advance notice warning to any bears that
might be close by so you do not take them by surprise. We also
advise everyone to carry bear spray in case of an encounter with
a bear. Outdoorsmen should also be on the watch for signs of
fresh bear activity, and be able to tell the difference between

black bear feces and grizzly bear feces. Black bear feces are small and contain lots of berries and squirrel fur. Grizzly shit has bells in it and smells like pepper spray.

Food Prep and Storage

In bear country, never keep or prepare food at your tent. A designated wilderness campsite will have a food prep and storage area with a fire ring several hundred feet from the tent sites. Do all of your cooking, eating, cleaning, and food storage in that area. If you are in a place where you can make your own campsite, follow the same practice of separating your sleeping and eating quarters.

All food, cookware, utensils, and trash—as well as any scented items such as toothpaste—should be bagged and then secured so a bear cannot easily get to them. Some campsites might have heavy metal bear boxes. Most sites use a bear pole—a high timber mounted between two trees. Hoist your bagged food to the top with the rope you brought with you. If there is no bear pole in place, look for a high branch protruding at least ten feet from a tree to mimic a bear pole apparatus.

Mountain Lions

I seriously doubt you will ever see one of these magnificent creatures. They are secretive, stealthy, and nocturnal. Infrequently, there are stories of a big cat ambushing and killing a human—always a solitary trail runner or walker or a separated child. Do not hike alone. Trail running is not a good idea. Keep young children close; in the wild, the young and vulnerable of any species are every predator's favorite prey. Do not hike at night.

Whereas bears are much bigger and stronger than you are and are not impressed by your bravado, you might frighten off a mountain lion—or at least convince the animal that an attack is not worthwhile. Stand tall. Act aggressively. Throw rocks and sticks. Be loud. Again, never run.

Once, while fossil hunting in the North Sulphur River, I stopped to eat lunch at the mouth of a feeder creek. While I sat quietly, two young mountain lions spilled out of the woods, playing and tussling down the gentle bank to the creek. These were no bobcats; these almost-grown adolescents were much bigger than any bobcat. After a minute, they noticed me (not twenty-five yards away) and stopped curiously. They looked at me for a moment, looked at each other, and then quickly (but with little concern) disappeared back into the woods. The encounter was really cool. Nonetheless, I got my stuff together and moved on to another hunting place. If the siblings came back with a mamma, the three would have me seriously outnumbered.

Snakes

I have seen far more snakes in my own backyard than I have in the sum total of my wilderness hikes. Still, you could run into a snake. Try not to. Stay on the trail instead of wandering through fallen wood and tall grass. Don't put your hands or feet (or your face!) into places where you cannot see. If you have some need to turn over rocks or woodpiles, use a stick. (Besides, there might be spiders or scorpions in those places too—and they creep me out much worse than snakes do.) Scan sunny, warm rock ledges carefully. If you see a snake, back off and let it slither away. Don't get curious about or play with the thing. Let it go away. The snake wants to get away from you as badly as you (should) want to get away from the snake.

I do come across snakes quite often when fossil hunting. As long as I see them first and there is a distance of several feet between us, I have become comfortable simply herding them out of the way. If a snake surprises me, I usually scream like a little girl and jump...then sheepishly calm down and herd it away. When in areas where I know I am likely to encounter snakes, I wear knee-high snake boots (or thick, thigh-high waders) and carry a shovel or a walking stick with which I poke ahead, turn over rocks, and herd snakes.

I was wading in a creek near downtown Fort Worth one day, looking for fossils, when I saw a frenetically writhing globe of snakes the diameter of a car tire in the water less than ten feet from me. Were there five snakes? Ten snakes? Fifty snakes? Was this a snake orgy? Snake WrestleMania? A snake death star? I had no idea, but I got out of the water.

If someone is bitten by a snake, you will have to get medical attention for that person. Many snakebites are "dry" (no venom is injected), but you cannot take the chance. Even the bite of a nonpoisonous snake can easily become infected or cause an allergic reaction.

According to a University of Florida–Johnson Lab report, updated in 2012 for the Department of Wildlife and Conservation by Dr. Steve A. Johnson, there are (on average) seven thousand to eight thousand venomous snakebites in the United States each year, and (on average) only five or six are fatal. You are very likely to live, but you do need to get medical attention.

There are some common dos and don'ts for snakebites. Don't apply a tourniquet, cold packs, or any type of suction device. Don't attempt to cut or suck the bite area. Don't raise the bite area above the head or heart. Don't let the person eat or drink anything.

Do calm the person down and restrict his or her movement. Keep the bite area level with or slightly below his or her heart. Let the bite bleed freely for thirty seconds or so before cleaning it. Remove anything (jewelry, tight clothing) that might restrict swelling. Do your best to recall the details of what the snake looked like. Do create a loose splint to restrict movement in the affected area. Carry the person out or help him or her out slowly, avoiding as much strenuous activity on his or her part as possible. Call a doctor or get medical attention as soon as possible.

Other Animals

Give any wild animal plenty of space. Do not intentionally interact with or approach wild animals. Never feed animals in the wild. Being trampled by a bison or an elk, charged by a moose, butted by a mountain goat, or even bitten by a cute, furry marmot will ruin your day. You are a visitor to their home. Be a respectful guest who leaves them alone. Watch warily and quietly from a distance. Let them go about their business, and then you can go about your business.

Surprises

The most startling creature I have ever encountered along the trail was a nearly foot-long slug in the rainforest ecosystem of Olympic National

Park. I had no idea such a thing existed. I also had no idea if it was poisonous or might have other superpowers. I got some pictures and was careful not to touch it. After returning home, I did some research. The thing was a banana slug, and, apparently, there are millions of them in that part of Olympic National Park.

Horrifically, they do have bizarre superpowers and habits. According to some researchers who claim to have witnessed such feats, they can climb and then drop from a tree while tethered from a slime string. A foot-long slug dropping on my shoulder would give me a heart attack. Although the slugs are hermaphrodites (having both male and female reproductive organs), they do need a partner in order to mate. When mating, a penis—which can be as long as the slug's entire body—emerges from the head of each slug. (I do not have a vivid enough imagination to visualize that scene.) Then, the act of mating (which I do not really understand either) lasts for hours. Afterward, the two slugs devour each other's penises, which must be nature's way of limiting the size of the slug population. The appendages do not grow back. Fortunately, I did not suffer the emotional scarring of witnessing such a mating event.

Sealock bet me that I could not work the word "penis" into this book in an innocuous, scientific, Dr. Spock sort of manner. Now that I have shared this fascinating—and true—information about banana slugs, he owes me a bottle of scotch.

These slugs are so beloved in the Pacific Northwest that there is an annual festival at Russian River, California, dedicated to them. The festival features slug races and a slug recipe contest. Having seen one of these things in the wild, I can tell you now that I will not eat one.

Kids

Children did not happen in my life, but I have spent a great deal of time with kids and young adults in camps, educational settings, and ministries. Maybe I have an interesting perspective for the parents among you, or maybe you'll write me off as someone who has never raised a child.

Remember the first rule: enjoy the wilderness experience! When you have kids in tow, the question is not what you would enjoy, nor is it what you want your kids to enjoy. The question is what your kids *might actually* enjoy.

If you want your kids to grow to love something, then help them—in stages—to become successful at that thing. Start small and grow. Introduce them at a level appropriate to their physical and mental maturity. Build their confidence with good experiences and successes and then introduce them to challenges that are more significant. Start with day hikes, camping at or near the car, or with a touristy visit to a national park. Introduce your children to the wilderness before you immerse them in it. I know your kid is special...isn't everyone's? But listen, I am trying to do you and your kid(s) a favor here.

The trail on our way out from a backpacking trip was every bit of ten miles. We had made the hard climb up and over a range from a mountain lake, which involved walking a good five miles while consistently gaining altitude. We stopped for lunch on the lake side of the ridge with a beautiful, long view of where we had spent the last several days. While we were resting and eating, a youngish father with his two very young boys, walking in from the road and trailhead, stopped to join us. The boys might have been eight and ten—maybe even younger. They had already walked the five miles in from the trailhead to this spot. The boys were miserably worn out. The dad was already worn down too; because the boys were too small to carry much in their miniature packs, he was loaded down like a horse. The three were visibly relieved to catch sight of their lake destination. It looked so beautiful and so close! We tried to think of some nondeflating way to tell them that the spectacular lake was still another five miles away.

As our group got ready to leave, I took the dad aside to tell him how far the trail led on, and to impress upon him the fact that this trail was much more strenuous getting out than going in. Turning back to the car might be a wise choice. He was at a decision point. Once they got some distance down the ridge, turning back would be harder than plowing on. I understood that he was trying to be father of year and give his kids a great adventure, but in my opinion, these kids were too young for that trail.

We don't know what happened. If the dad and his boys did turn back, they would not have been able to catch up to our pace. I am sure they survived, and I am sure that they had a story to tell; I just hope it was a good one. Maybe the dad made men out of his boys. But more likely, he made them never want to walk a trail again.

My rule for kids and backpacking is simple. If a kid is not big enough and old enough to carry his or her own stuff, then he/she is not ready for a backpacking trip. There are many other options for wilderness fun. Find a hike and campsite that's a mile or two from the car but still feels like backpacking to them.

There is another problem with kids—especially with boys—and backpacking (or long day hikes). Young males have an innate compulsion to do reckless, thoughtless things. That propensity is not a good attribute ten miles into the backcountry and far from any help or services whatsoever.

An interesting parallel story. The largest mammoth dig in the United States is in Hot Springs, South Dakota. Sealock and I visited the place in a meandering road trip to one of our own adventures. Twenty-six thousand years ago, the now excavated area was a sinkhole (a thin limestone covering collapsed into a cave) with a natural breccia pipe allowing geothermally warmed spring water to percolate up and fill the hole. The result was a large, warm-water, very steep-sided (below the waterline) pond that existed for some five hundred years before silting over. The warm water created lush vegetation. Attracted by the warm water and vegetation, mammoths would wander into the pond and then could not gain enough footing to get out, due to the steep sides. The animals would die of exhaustion, starvation, or drowning. A few predators, giant short-faced bears and saber-toothed cats, attracted by the stranded meat, would also occasionally become trapped and die. To date, sixty-one mammoth remains (a couple of woollies and the rest Columbian) have been uncovered. Here's the thing. Practically all of the remains belong to the equivalent of teenage or young adult males. The older females leading the herd groups were wise enough to stay away from the place. The younger females were smart enough to listen to their elders. The adult males, who had already managed to survive their own adolescence, had finally learned a thing or two (the hard way, probably). The adolescent and young males, of course, thought they could handle this odd pond just fine. You can now enjoy viewing their fragile bones (twenty-five thousand years is far too little time for bones to fossilize).

Keep a watchful eye on boys and young adults in the wilderness—the caution function in their brains just does not work right yet.

The situation is more difficult if you have more than one boy to keep up with. There was an elder in my church who was one of the finest men I have ever known. He was a brilliant engineer and chief executive officer of a company, and he was the husband, father, and grandfather that every guy should aspire to be. (I was privileged to know you, Bob McDonald.)

Bob also loved working with his hands on all kinds of woodworking projects. One day, after I knew that his grandboys (three of them, aged eight to eleven) had been visiting for the weekend, I asked Bob how the boys did at helping him with his projects.

"Well," Bob said thoughtfully, as always, "when it comes to help, a boy is worth about a boy. Two boys are less than half a boy. Three boys are no boy at all."

Your kids (boys and girls) really are great. You can help them to love the outdoors. Just take it easy with them and help them to make good decisions until they grow into loving the activity on their own. That way, they will be leading *you* farther down the trail before you know it.

Places I Have Pooped

f you walk a ways in the wilderness, eventually you will have to relieve yourself. Shit happens—on a somewhat regular basis, if you are a healthy person. What is the process and etiquette for properly taking care of your personal business along the trail?

Before we step right into that messy business, a quick note. Sitting around a campfire one night with nothing else to do on one of our backpacking trips, Sealock and I came up with the idea of creating and selling a coffee-table book full of breathtakingly beautiful pictures of natural scenery titled (like this chapter) *Places I Have Pooped*. The idea is ours; we have not implemented the plan, but now that I have put the idea in print, you may not steal it.

Every national or state wilderness area you might hike in has rules about your potty habits on the trail. Do some research: read the online information or read the books about the area you planning to explore. Although I am not aware of anyone ever being arrested for infractions of such rules, please be as respectful and decent as possible. While bear or mountain lion scat along a trail is worthy of interest and inspection, your shit is not all that great or appreciated.

Generally, the rules and etiquette for relieving yourself boil down to a few simple concepts. Walk at least one hundred yards from any creek, wash area, or water source, as well as at least one hundred yards from any trail or campsite before doing your business. Dig a hole. (U-Dig-It makes a great collapsible shovel tool in a sheath that attaches to your belt for this and many other useful purposes.) Do your business in the hole you just dug. Bury your biodegradable toilet paper in the hole. Cover the hole with dirt and stomp it down. Then, carry on with your day. Peeing is a relatively simple and quick process, especially if you are a guy. However, you still should dig a small hole to pee in and then cover it with dirt; apparently, animals are attracted to licking up the salts in your pee otherwise.

Many national parks, understandably concerned about human impact on the wilderness areas they protect, provide wilderness toilets at the permitted, designated backcountry campsites. These potty stations—which you are required to use at designated campsites—vary wildly and dramatically in appearance and functionality (even within the same park). Perhaps the government is running some long-term experiment. Many such contraptions are highly successful magnets for every fly, mosquito, and other annoying insect for twenty square miles. I would much rather dig a hole elsewhere in the woods in peace, but using the wilderness toilet is the rule.

Once, in Glacier National Park, while camping along the upper Quartz Lakes, we pitched our tents, made camp, and (as always) walked down the signed footpath to inspect the state of the designated wilderness toilet. We were stunned. This thing was the nicest wilderness toilet we had ever seen (ignoring, of course, the fact that there was a giant pile of decaying feces and urine beneath it). Many of these toilets are built in an open-air, potty-stool design with no walls or door. This beauty was a tiny house made of cedar. It even still smelled like cedar. My wife would have allowed a cedar closet designed like this in our house (sans the giant pile below, of course). We felt like we had checked into the Waldorf Astoria.

Later that evening, while contemplating life in this lovely cedar abode, I did notice two unusual characteristics of its splendid design. First, there were bolt locks on both the outside and on the inside of the door. These locks were not for privacy issues. Signage inside and out reminded visitors to bolt the inside lock when using the facility and to remember to bolt the outside lock when they leave the facility. Glacier is bear country, after all. When you go to the bathroom in Glacier, do not forget your toilet paper...or your bear spray. The second thing I noticed was also bear related—another sign imploring me *never* to dump food remains in the toilet ("big hole in the ground" would have been a better description). So, I sat for a while and wondered just what sort of bear would scavenge through a big pile of crap just to find a few leftover chili mac noodles.

Along the trails, there are (thankfully), no wilderness toilets. Discreetly walk away an appropriate distance, dig your hole, and do your business. Glacier, once again, was the scene of one my favorite long day hikes—the fourteen-mile Highline trail from Logan's Pass to the bus stop at the midway point of Going to the Sun Road. Halfway along the trail is the Granite Chalet. If you are not an idiot (we met a few on the trail who had started at the bottom and walked up all day), you start your hike at the top of the continental divide at the pass and then work your way down. More than half of the hike is well above the tree line. We were on the trail by 7:00 a.m. We'd had a big breakfast to be fueled for the day. And I had already started eating snacks. I needed to go. In fact, I had needed to go for several miles—but there was not a tree or bush or discreet potty area in sight. Getting off the narrow trail up or down meant navigating a forty-five degree to sixty-degree slope. Finally, we got to a place where I saw three scraggly bushes 150 yards below. I really had to go. I told Mike to distract anyone who happened along the trail.

"What is this," he said, "the Wizard of Oz? You want me to tell them to ignore the man squatting behind the little bushes?"

"Just wing it," I said, and then hurried off. I slid down to the bushes. I dug my hole (not an easy task on a hard rock mountainside). As I finally assumed the awkward squatting position, I heard Sealock loudly chatting up someone on the trail. Then, glancing to my left, I saw some pink earbuds on the ground; apparently, I was not the first human being to discover these bushes. As I finished, a horrible realization swept over me; in my haste to reach the bushes, I had left my toilet paper in my day pack on the trail. Damn. Improperly cleaning oneself when walking long distances can create quite uncomfortable rashes. Just trust me on this advice. The leaves on these pitiful bushes were not going to do me any good. What I did have was an old, tie-dyed bandanna that I was wearing around my head as a do-rag. The bandanna had sentimental value to me, but the need was dire. I dutifully bagged the befouled and less-than-biodegradable bandanna and scrambled back up to the trail. Mike looked at me quizzically for a minute and said, "Did you lose your do-rag?"

"You don't want to know," I replied. Being a great friend and an excellent hiking buddy, he left the conversation at that. Much later that night, when we were unpacking our stuff and getting ready for the next day, I came across the ziplock bag with my desecrated bandanna. I explained the trash to Mike and asked if he thought I could wash and save the item, which really did have some sentimental value to me. He looked at me as if I had finally lost my mind and offered no opinion.

To research much more fully the history, art, and etiquette of taking care of your personal business in the wilderness, please find *How to Shit in the Woods*, by Kathleen Meyer, an excellent book now in its third edition.

Guns

When conversations turn to backpacking or hiking, people who have never walked a mile away from a road often say, "You carry a gun, don't you?"

My answer is no. Your answer might be different.

I have nothing against guns. I am very glad that I learned some gun and hunting skills as a young man; but frankly, after the initial rush, realizing that I did not actually have to kill in order to eat put a damper on my interest in hunting. I understand that hunting can be a fun and challenging interest or hobby, but shooting creatures just did not become my thing.

I have a couple of hunting firearms even though I don't need them. I am not a commando, nor am I disposed to pretending to be one or to arming myself like one. Brandishing a firearm does not make me feel particularly cool or safe. My job as a consultant to non-profits and churches (unlike being a rancher who must protect his livestock, for instance) does not necessitate my being armed. I do not anticipate fending off a zombie apocalypse. Handguns are not much good for anything except shooting people quite near you—something that I have no inclination to do. I certainly have no need for armor-piercing bullets and automatic weapons. Some people, however, really like guns—including many law-abiding people in gun-crazy America who do not need them for any rational purpose. As far as I am concerned, that is OK. I also buy all kinds of crap that I don't really need; that is how the American economy works. I also collect fossils—as if anyone needs those!

The reasons I do not carry a gun on the trail are practical rather than idealistic or political:

1. Guns and ammunition are very heavy. Discarding unnecessary weight is paramount for backpacking trips or long day hikes.
2. In more than thirty years of walking trails, wilderness areas, national parks, rivers, creeks, and other wilder areas, I have not encountered any situation in which a gun would have been even remotely useful to me.
3. The most likely outcome of carrying and discharging a handgun is that I accidently injure (or kill) myself or someone else. Another outcome is that I purposely kill myself or someone else. Somehow, saving the world—or even myself—with a gun is way down the list of likely occurrences. Simply put, I can find no compelling rationale for carrying a heavy, potential accident around.
4. If you are worried about bears or wolves or mountain lions or wild hogs or whatever, there are other effective precautions you can take. First and always, use your enormous brain to your advantage. Know how to be aware, how to avoid problems, and how to react. Bear spray—lightweight, easy to carry, and simple to aim and deploy—is more effective than any small firearm you might carry. Shooting a bear with a handgun is as likely to enrage as to dissuade the animal. Yes, dangerous animal encounters do very rarely happen; but aside from questionable human decision making, dangerous encounters are extremely unlikely.
5. Human beings managed to survive in and conquer a dangerous world for thousands of years before guns (or bear sprays) were invented. You will likely survive your backpack trip without a gun.

Carry a gun if you wish. Remember, just because you can carry a gun into a one of these areas does not mean that you (legally or otherwise) have the right to shoot at stuff or animals randomly just because you feel like it. If you want to play with your guns, then go hunting or shooting in a designated hunting or shooting area.

Admittedly, I was not pleased when guns were allowed in national parks. I am much more concerned about people wandering around the parks with guns than I am about bears going about their business. The most dangerous animals to worry about in any neck of any woods are other people. That thought almost makes me want to carry a gun.

Planning Ahead for Backcountry Permits in National Parks

<hr />

All national parks require permits for backpacking routes and backcountry designated campsites. Of course, some parks are busier than others are, and the permitting processes and time frames vary considerably.

What does not vary is the significant amount of advance research and planning you will need to do to determine the route you want to take and to choose specific campsites. Let's say you want to walk in six miles and stay the first two nights at a particular mountain lake. There may be two or four or six designated campsites around that lake. Campfires may be allowed at some sites and not others. Some sites may allow four tents and some may allow only two tents. Sites have limits on the number of nights they can be reserved and the dates they are open. Sealock wants to make fire. I don't particularly want nearby neighbors. So, our first choice might be a somewhat isolated campsite with a fire pit and room for only two tents for two nights. Then we have to figure out our second, third, and fourth choices for that night. You need to know what you prefer, in detail and in order, before filling out an itinerary for a permit. In fact, you will need to know the details for two or three different itineraries because the application allows you to submit a second- and third-choice trip in case your primary route is not available. There will be an application fee, ranging from ten to sixty dollars.

Go to the website of the national park you are planning to visit. Click the "plan your visit" tab, the "things to do" tab, and then the "backcountry camping" tab to find the information you need. There will be links to campsite maps and availability, application forms, and a tutorial on how to use the form. *Pay attention to the mode of application, payment, and the dates for submission.* Some parks only accept applications electronically. Some parks require mailed or faxed applications. Dates for receiving and reviewing applications also vary considerably. For example, as I write, Glacier National Park will not take applications until March 15, 2017, for summer trips. Yellowstone National Park will receive applications starting January 1, 2017, but will not begin reviewing and processing applications until March 31. Both will continue to review applications on a first come, first served basis, up to ten days before your trip. However, the longer you wait to apply, the less likely your first choices will be available. All parks operate on a first come, first served basis. Very few parks are so lightly used that last-minute planning is advisable.

You can go to a national park, walk into a ranger station with no plan at all, and ask for a backpacking permit. You will get whatever happens to be leftover that day due to no-shows, cancellations, and any excess capacity. There is a possibility you will get something, but you will have no (or few) choices about where or for how long you can backpack. You will have no control over or how hard a trail you hike, where you will camp, or how many days your trek can last. I strongly suggest getting your preferred choices into the application queue as early as that park's policies allow.

Sealock and I generally figure out our vacation schedule around the first of the year, choose a destination and research several itineraries, make our travel arrangements (air travel at reasonable cost is always the hassle that determines the specific days we can backpack), and then get our backcountry application in as soon as the park policy allows. By doing so, we usually get our first choice, and we have never been bumped past our second choice.

Get a good hiking book (like a *Falcon Guide*) for the area you are interested in with detailed descriptions of each trail. Get a Trails Illustrated topographical map. Do some research on the park website. You will have to download the park's backcountry campsite resource to get the coded information and regulations for designated campsites along your route. Pick the trails and route you would like to explore, choose the campsites you prefer, and determine an itinerary and a daily schedule. Repeat the process with a different set of trails and campsites. Now you are ready to fill out and submit an application.

If you get your application in early, you may have to wait of a month or more before receiving an itinerary-confirmation e-mail. Be patient. Calling the ranger station will not speed up the process. Eventually, you will receive an e-mail confirming your itinerary. This confirmation is not your permit. The e-mail will contain instructions for how and when you can pick up your actual permits when you arrive for your adventure. Keep the confirmation e-mail! Print a copy and bring that confirmation to the ranger station to pick up your permits.

It is possible that you will arrive at the ranger station to pick up your permits, confirmed itinerary in hand and ready to go, only to find that your route has been closed because of lingering snowpacks, unusual bear activity, or some other unforeseen circumstance. The rangers will already have other itinerary options available for you and will help you to choose the alternate route that best fits your wishes. Please remember that these changes are made with your safety and well-being in mind. The few times plans had to change, I have always found the park service and the rangers to be helpful and accommodating.

Trail Eve and Day

Plan to stay the afternoon and evening before your backpacking trip at a hotel or campsite relatively close to your trailhead. Know where you can find and purchase any last-minute items such as matches, lighters, camp-stove fuel, bear spray, fishing licenses, or extra food. If you are in an area that requires permits for backpacking and camping (as most national parks do), go to the ranger station to pick up your permits early and to get up-to-date information about your route.

The night before your trip, have everyone in the group lay out all of the stuff he or she plans to carry. Go over each item together to make sure that people in your group have what they need. Even more importantly, weed out redundant or unnecessary items. Over the next several days, you will be happy that you lightened your load. For example, your group of four people does not need four saws, four sets of cookware, and four rarely used tools. Pare down one last time, and then organize your pack for the trail. The next morning, you want to just put your pack on and go. Go ahead and pack up the car. Drink lots of water and not much alcohol.

Get going early on trail day. Eat a hearty breakfast. Fill up your water bottles and containers. Visit the last real toilet you will see for days.

If required—and if you have not already done so—go to the ranger station to pick up a parking permit (leave it on the windshield dash of your car at the trailhead), camping permits (attach them to your tents at the campsite), and fishing permits. You may be required to watch a bear and safety video before receiving your permits. Always ask the rangers for trail and weather conditions, bear and other animal activity, recommended side trips, and so on. Visit a semireal toilet again.

By the way, rangers *do* regularly check permits and campsites in national parks. We have seen people being told to pack up their stuff and marched all the way back to the trailhead because they thought they could skip or skirt the backcountry permitting process. I do not know if they were fined too, but the long trek back was plenty of punishment.

Drive to the trailhead, lock up your car, and be sure to remember where in your pack you carefully stashed the keys. Say good-bye to cell phones, plumbing, roads, cars, buildings, lights, and people. Time for a cool change. Get your pack on, strap up, start walking, take some deep breaths...and enjoy! Within minutes, and for the next several days, you will be in a different world.

How to Pack Your Backpack

Everyone develops his or her own personal organizational system, I suppose, but some tips I have learned might be helpful for you. Essentially, you want to avoid having to dig through your whole pack randomly (and then repack it) every time you need an item.

Repackage what you can into smaller, lighter containers. For example, you do not need the cracker or snack boxes or plastic. Just put the amount of food you want into a ziplock bag. The elaborate packaging that most stuff comes in is just more trash and weight for you to carry around.

Make creative use of dead or empty spaces. For example, my little gas-stove set, foldable spork, matches, lighter, and camp soap will fit *inside* my nested set of two pots.

Arrange heavier items and items that you only use at the campsite (such as cookware, stove, most food, and sleeping bag) at the bottom of your pack.

Stuff all of your clothes into one stuff sack (except for a heavy shirt and your rain gear) so they are easy to find. I also use this stuff sack as my pillow.

Make sure that a warm shirt and your rain gear are very easily accessible (usually at the top of your pack) for quick retrieval along the trail.

Package your lunch for the day and some trail snacks in the side pockets or quick-access top position of your pack.

Put all the rest of your food into one stuff sack (or into a heavy-duty trash bag or an extralarge ziplock) so it is easy to find and ready to tie up on the bear pole.

Use various, easy-access side pockets for items you may retrieve often, such as sunscreen, bug spray, binoculars, trail snacks, water-purification pump, trail map, wilderness toilet paper, and a bandanna.

Attach your small camera and case to your shoulder strap. You will use the camera so often that you won't want to have to dig it out.

Keep a knife in your pocket.

Attach your bear spray to your belt—don't stash it somewhere that's not easily accessible! Your personal, folding potty digger can also be attached to your belt.

Attach large, weatherproof items such as your tent, sleeping pad, and perhaps a rolled tarp to the outside of your pack with small bungee cords. (These little cords have a multitude of good uses!) Most packs have additional straps and loops for this purpose. Avoid stacking and tying items to the top of your pack. Besides looking silly, large items stacked or dangling at the top of your pack put the pack (and, thus, you) awkwardly out of balance.

Personally, I place my sleeping bag inside my pack because I never want it to get wet. If you strap your sleeping bag outside your pack, be sure to waterproof it by placing it into a heavy-duty trash bag.

Loose, dangling things half-strapped all over your pack will be constantly annoying.

If you cannot get everything except your tent, sleeping pad, and perhaps a small tarp secured inside your pack (or in side pockets), then you are likely carrying too much stuff.

Do not forget your (full) water bottles! Most packs, even those with hydration systems, have mesh side pockets at the hip for water bottles.

In a small, interior pocket of you pack, put your driver's license, medical insurance card, a credit card, and some cash (perhaps a fifty-dollar bill). You will likely need none of that, but you certainly do not need more of a wallet or purse than that.

By the way, the combination of altitude, wearing a pack, and walking long distances with your hands mostly down at your sides will make your hands swell. This is quite normal. It's best to leave jewelry—including rings—at home. I learned this lesson the hard way one year. My hands were a bit swollen, as usual, at the start of the hike. Then I slightly jammed my ring finger, which was no big deal, except that I could not get my wedding band off. A little more swelling suddenly became problematic. I thought I might have to file the ring off with the small file tool on my Swiss Army knife. Fortunately, practically freezing my hand in a cold stream for a while took the swelling down enough to avoid that task.

Coming Off the Trail

From experience, I would strongly suggest that you plan an evening of downtime at the end of the trail. Walking hurriedly off a backpacking trail, getting in your car, and trying to make a flight or drive home that evening is unnecessarily stressful. There are too many variables in timing; you never know what the weather or other circumstances might be, and you are going to be tired.

Factor an evening of downtime into the trip. Get a good hotel room, and ask for a lot of extra towels and shampoo. Enjoy the luxuries of a real toilet and a shower. Go out on the town, eat a big dinner with fresh ingredients, do some fun tourist things. Have a beer or a scotch. Back at the hotel, enjoy a real toilet again (maybe read a paper and catch up on the news, since you have been off the grid for a week). Get a good night's sleep in a real bed with a real pillow.

Adjusting to reality after a week in the wilderness may take a few days. Civilization is great, but it's also noisy, bright, and frenetic. And there are other people everywhere.

Coming back from New Mexico one year, my wife picked Mike and me up at the airport. We had been out for six days and had conversed with few people during that time. Of course, we talked with each other...sometimes...generally somewhat quietly and in no hurry. We were not quite prepared for Lisa's verbal exuberance to catch us up on an entire week. I thought Mike was going to bail out of the car along the interstate.

On another trip home from Colorado, Mike decided to drive our rental car back to Colorado Springs from the trailhead. I am not sure why. I always drove, mainly because I usually had travel points that could be converted to free rental car days. I should have known this change of habit was a bad idea when he backed into a giant boulder three seconds into our trip. The damage was barely noticeable, so we ventured on with Sealock at the wheel. Beth was soon asleep in the back seat. Winding down a steep, curvy mountain road, Mike decided to shift the automatic drive into a lower gear for engine braking. Somehow, though, he actually shifted into reverse. The car shook violently, lurched a few dozen feet down the mountain road, and then shut itself down. Every warning light and dinging alarm on the entire dashboard went off simultaneously. The ignition would no longer work.

"Oops," he said. Then, after a long pause, he asked, "Any idea on what we should do now?"

I had no real clue, but my Male Answer Syndrome quickly kicked in. "Just turn the key off. Let it sit for a while, and maybe it will forget about the whole thing," I said. "Maybe it will just reboot."

We sat for five minutes without saying anything because 1) Beth was still sleeping and snoring in the back, and 2) neither of us had a better idea. When Mike tried the ignition again, the car started up; the warning lights cycled on one more time and then quit, and we drove on to Colorado Springs. Walking is so much simpler, but we had a long way to go.

The People You Will Meet

***

Truthfully, part of the reason I backpack is to get away from most people. We might not see another person for days after getting on a trail. I don't dislike people; I just don't need a lot of them around. You will, however, meet a lot of (mostly) nice and interesting people as you travel into our national parks and wilderness areas. Spend some time talking with a ranger. Visit with the retired, volunteer rangers who spend their summers at the park. Talk to the servers and staff at the national park lodges and restaurants—most of them are foreign exchange students with interesting perspectives and stories about why they wanted to spend time in America's parklands. Visit with the scoutmaster and the troop on the bus to the trail. Get the real scoop on winter from the locals at the diner or the bar. I have always wanted to talk to the crews who clear the roads of millions of tons of snow in the spring. The variety of people in our national parks is fascinating—young, old, wealthy, no money whatsoever, bikers, hippies, students, retirees, families, tourists, and backpackers. You will encounter people from all walks of life, but most everyone seems to find common ground in these beautiful, wild places. You will be stunned by how many people from all over the world visit our national parks. I understand their interest; if I were visiting America, these are the places I would want to see too.

Occasionally, you will share the trail or lunch or dinner or a campsite with a few people. Be a friendly American and a good neighbor. Share. Be helpful. No one walks a trail hoping to meet an ass.

One year in the Pecos Wilderness, Sealock and I had set up camp in a lovely valley near a stream that fed the Pecos River. We fished in the late afternoon. Mike had about a thousand dollars' worth of fancy fly-fishing gear. I had a two-foot, collapsible, children's Zebco rod from Walmart that came with some crappie spinners. We both caught fish—though Sealock did look much cooler than I did. We had carried in a six-pack of beer (our heavy splurge item for the trip) and chilled it under a big rock in the river. We made a fire, got out the grate, and started cooking fresh trout while drinking ice-cold beer. Mike was tending to the trout while I enjoyed a beer in my hammock. About that time, a fiftyish dad and his twentyish son wandered into our camp. They were returning to their nearby campsite from a day hike and smelled our dinner. They looked a little haggard and somewhat stunned to see us enjoying cold beer and fresh fish. We invited them to dinner (there was plenty of fish), gave them each a beer, and spent an enjoyable evening visiting and laughing together. They did ask if they could go camping with us next time.

On an awesome trip, eight of us trekked across the Continental Divide and down the Bechler River in Yellowstone. We literally put on our packs at Old Faithful and then walked to Idaho. The night before we started on the trail, we ate dinner at the park's famous old lodge.

On a lark, Mike went to the reception desk to ask about getting a room. Two of the clerks busted out laughing, saying, "Man, you have to get reservation two years in advance for a room here."

Then the third host said, "Wait! There's a cancellation." The three women in our party got a nice room with a shower. We five guys were still stuck in the tiny bunk-bed cabin that we had reserved.

As we were getting ready to put the packs on at Old Faithful the next morning, we noticed that one person was missing. He was an old friend of Mike's whom I had not met before this trip. He was a good-natured and talkative sort of fellow. We finally spotted him surrounded by a gnarly looking biker gang, having some kind of animated conversation. Mike motioned for me to go over with him and help. In my head, like any Lord of the Rings fan, I was thinking, "So it begins."

Mike has been seriously practicing some kind of kung fu-ish stuff for many years. I guess his whole body is a weapon now. Me? I was looking for a big stick. We have never been in a brawl together. We are both the slow-to-anger type. I like to imagine that we both could account for ourselves quite well, if we needed to. But then again, we might just be thrashed.

When we walked up, the biggest (really big) biker said gruffly, "Are you friends of this guy?"

"Yes," Mike bravely volunteered. I wasn't sure I knew the guy well enough to be a friend just yet.

"Y'all going walking out there for days?" he asked and pointed vaguely. "Ain't you afraid of running into a bear or something?"

"Well," Mike replied, "I was actually more worried about running into something like...er...you."

They all laughed, and we talked awhile about their motorcycle club and their trip and about backpacking. They wished us well, and we started walking.

At the end of that same trip, we walked to a ranger station in Idaho where Mike had previously parked a rental car. There were eight of us with lots of gear. The car was an SUV, but there was no way we would all fit into it. I still can't believe seven of them did fit. They could drive straight to Jackson Hole (where we would all fly out), but I had to get back to Old Faithful, where my rental car was parked. I had joined them after a business trip to—and a long drive from—Sun Valley, Idaho. My friends were certainly willing to take me back to my car, but the offer was ridiculously (four hours or more) out of their way. I decided to see if I could hitchhike back to Old Faithful.

There were only three cars at this ranger station/trailhead. The people in the first car were not heading back to Yellowstone (so they said, rather dismissively). The people near the second car looked at me as though I were some kind of (very dirty after six days on the trail) deranged serial killer and quickly left without saying anything. In the third car, a small van, were four college students headed back to the center of Yellowstone. My offer of fifty dollars for gas (remember when I said to put a fifty-dollar bill in your backpack?) meant a lot to them. I had a ride. There was no room in a seat for me, so I lay on top of all the gear in the back of the van.

An hour into our drive, my phone rang. I had been waiting for a signal to call home, since I had not talked to my wife in almost a week. It was Lisa.

"Hey!" she said. "Mike called me to say y'all were off the trail safe, but when I asked him to pass the phone to you, he said you weren't there, and then the call dropped. Everything OK?"

"Yes, we had a great trip! Everything good with you?"

"All good. Glad y'all are safe. Pass the phone over to Katy (Beth's youngest daughter) and let me ask how the trip *really* was."

"She's not here."

"What do you mean she's not there?"

"They are in the rental car, headed back to Jackson Hole."

There was a long pause. "Well, where are you?"

"In a van headed back to Yellowstone to get my rental car."

"What van? Whose van?"

"I don't know."

"What do you mean you don't know?"

"I don't really know their names or anything…some college kids from the University of Washington. I had to hitch a ride back to my car at Old Faithful. They seem like nice people."

"Jesus!" she exclaimed. "How old are you?" (I was in my late forties, but Lisa knew that). "Well, put your seatbelt on and be careful," she said.

"I am lying in the back of a van on top of a bunch of backpacks. I don't think there is a seatbelt back here."

"Jesus," she said again.

"Honey, I don't know how long this signal is going to last, so let me call you back in a couple of hours when I get to my car at Old Faithful. Love you. Bye."

I spent the next several hours playing the ancient, wise sage to these college kids, who were spending the whole summer hitting national park trails. I called Lisa back to catch up and then bought my grasshoppers some beers at the Old Faithful Lodge. Then, I drove a couple of hours to meet my group in Jackson Hole. We ate a huge, late dinner in the cool little town, and then flew out the next morning. What a great trip. I sometimes wonder how those kids turned out and what they do now. I am pretty sure they have never thought about me again since that afternoon.

On the trail to the top of Half Dome in Yosemite, we ran into all kinds of characters. The most surprising was a young, Amish couple. She had the ankle-length dress and a bonnet on. He had the black slacks, suspenders, tie, and a black hat with a white shirt. They had already walked better than eight miles to the base of the last ascent in the most uncomfortable-looking dress shoes I had ever seen. I wanted to ask them how they got to Yosemite in the first place—in a buggy, maybe?

Halfway back down, late that same afternoon, Mike and I heard—rather than saw—a woman ahead of us on the trail. I thought she was yelling in Italian; Mike guessed it was French. We had no idea what she was saying, but clearly she was exceptionally unhappy and letting someone know about it. The tirade went on nonstop for five minutes, growing ever louder as we rounded a bend and saw the young woman animatedly lambasting her young man companion. When we passed them on the trail, she did not even pause for air. He just kept walking with his head down. She was nowhere near finished. We continued to hear her after we lost sight of them around another bend in the trail.

Then, suddenly, the avalanche of words stopped, and the wilderness was quiet again. I stopped and looked around quizzically, waiting for the vituperation to resume. "You think she finally ran out of steam?" I asked.

Mike shrugged. "I think he finally killed her."

One morning on a trip in Yellowstone, as Mike and I were about to leave our campsite for a daylong hike to the top of Mount Holmes, a middle-aged, very fit couple zoomed by on the trail, speed walking with trekking poles flying around in every hand. They clearly had no time or inclination to stop and chat. We decided they were German. She had those really annoying bear bells on and sounded like a sleigh ride at the pace they were going. Much later that morning, we saw them again at the far edge of a large Alpine meadow. We stopped awhile for snacks to avoid getting into jingle range and watched some elk move back into the meadow after the bells disappeared.

Quite mysteriously, we never saw the German couple again. As far as we knew—and as far as a good trail map showed—the only trail in the area led to the top of Mount Holmes and then back again, past our campsite. We had to work our way around several large snowpacks and then reacquire the trail to get to Mount Holmes. There were no footprints in the snow except ours. We did not see the couple coming down the mountain as we went up, nor did we see them at the top. We had been above tree line for several miles; there was no place to hide. Late that afternoon, halfway back to our campsite, I found some kind of fancy compass/navigation device alongside the trail. It was German-made, and it was broken. If they passed our campsite along the trail later that evening, then we missed them (and the damn bells) somehow. For several weeks after our trip, we looked for news articles about a German couple disappearing in Yellowstone. Nothing. The case remains a mystery.

In Glacier National Park one lovely afternoon, I was lying in my hammock ten feet from a beautiful, remote, glacial lake surrounded by mountains, whittling a walking stick. Mike had hiked down to a lower lake to try the fishing there. Although we were backpacking and camping at this site, the trail to this lake was sometimes used as a long day hike. As I whittled away, enjoying the sun and the view, a three-generation family made it to the lake. Norwegian? Swedish? Something Nordic. A stunningly handsome couple in their early forties, their two daughters (an early twenties supermodel and her sister, who was at that awkward age of maybe fourteen), and a grandma and grandpa. As soon as they saw the lake, the grandpa pulled out a camcorder and started filming.

The "beach access" for the lake was about five feet of sand and rock about five feet directly in front of my hammock. They dropped their gear right there in front of me, offering greetings in a language I did not understand. Grandpa filmed me smiling and waving back to them. Then, without a care in the world, mom and dad completely disrobed to go for a swim. She was even better looking than I had first thought. Then, the twenty-year-old took her clothes off. (Later, when relating this story, I told my wife that it had been many, many years since I had seen a naked twenty-year-old woman.) Grandpa was still filming everything while grandma clapped and shouted encouragement to the family. When the fourteen-year-old finally responded to her father's animated gestures to join in and started to take off her clothes, I had to swing out of the hammock and walk away; this scene was turning creepy for a prudish American. Besides, grandma was probably next.

When I returned, the naked Nordics were gone. I had just settled back into my hammock when a group of normally homely and overweight Americans arrived—two guys and three girls. I gave them a friendly wave, offering up a silent prayer that there would be no more nakedness this day.

When Mike returned later in the day, I told him that he had missed quite the show.

"What happened?" he asked.

"Well," I said, "when was the last time you saw a stunningly good-looking, naked, twenty-year-old woman?"

He looked bewildered. After regaining his composure, he said, "Whatever this story is, be sure to mention the fact that I was not there when you tell it again."

To begin a long, spectacularly beautiful day hike to Grinnell Glacier from the fabulous Many Glacier Hotel (which inspired Stephen King's *The Shining*), Sealock and I decided to take the old-fashioned, tourist boat across the first two lakes in the journey. Our tour guide was a college-age woman enjoying her summer job. Back in the day, I was such an ignorant-of-the-world college student that the availability of an awesome job like hers did not occur to me. Indeed, youth is wasted on (most of) the young.

There were about twenty other people on the restored wooden boat—some retirees, some families with kids, several visitors from outside the United States. After some introductory greetings and comments, our very informative tour guide pointed to the striking, piercing mountain feature dominating the view on the far side of the lake from the hotel. The mountain feature, carved by massive, moving glaciers on both sides, was a tall and incredibly steep geological wonder.

"Does anyone know what this kind of glacially carved feature is called?" she asked. No one responded. "This," she said dramatically, standing and pointing like Vanna White, "is a giant erection."

Mike and I start giggling like a couple of twelve-year-old boys. *Ha-ha...she said, "Giant erection."* We were both in our fifties at the time. No one else on the boat laughed or even smirked. I was thinking, *Really? This is funny! She is talking about a giant erection!* No one else showed any response at all. It was like a zombie boat. Mike and I couldn't stop laughing.

Our tour guide went on for more than five minutes, discussing giant erections. She talked about how giant erections are made, and then she described how difficult it was for anyone to climb on top of a giant erection. (I am not making this story up.) She was completely deadpan. No one else on the boat showed any visible reaction. Mike and I were trying not to wet ourselves, we were laughing so hard.

When she finally concluded her giant erection speech, I nudged Mike and said, "Listen, I am going to raise my hand for a question and then ask her to start over and repeat the whole giant erection thing so you can get it on video. Otherwise, no one will believe it."

Mike nixed that idea, reasoning that the request might be a bit immature. Besides, the completely unresponsive crowd was deflating the moment.

At the end of the boat ride, we quickly outpaced the zombie passengers and had a stunningly gorgeous hike and day to ourselves, walking up past more glacial lakes to a large, glacial cirque, all the while laughing about how to climb a giant erection. I actually know a few things about geology, but I had never heard of a giant erection. You should always learn something every day.

We walked back the hotel about 5:00 p.m. While having adult beverages on the hotel porch, we spotted the only grizzly bears we saw during that entire trip, a mother with her cub. They were across the lake from the hotel. We got an early seating for dinner at a window table in the lodge restaurant, a gem from the Roaring Twenties. Before we left, we toasted another great day in the outdoors—as well as the giant erection that loomed across the lake from us.

The Bad Trip (Or Was That a Flying Mountain Goat?)

Despite all of your planning, preparation, and good decisions, some outings turn unexpectedly difficult and uncomfortable—usually because of weather that you cannot control. A Bad Trip happens occasionally, and you just have to make the best of it.

One of our group trips to the Pecos Wilderness in New Mexico, with a couple of backpacking novices in tow, did not go according to plan. The trip started out great. We flew in and had a blast playing in Santa Fe for a day and an evening. Early the next morning, we stopped at a pancake house for breakfast, and Sealock ate some special pancake thing piled a foot high with fake-looking candied fruit bits and whipped cream. Driving out to the trailhead, we stopped by the ranger station to ask about conditions, current regulations, and bear activity, and to let the station know about our itinerary. The ranger told us not to worry about bears where we were going. The local drought had been so bad that the bears had come down from altitude and were foraging around the small town. Two bears had busted into the local doughnut shop the night before.

The morning hike was great, except that Mike could not stop hiccupping and burping up breakfast. We stopped in an alpine meadow for a long lunch. After we got back on the trail, things went downhill. The weather changed dramatically and quickly. Rain came down hard and cold. Pretty much for the next three days, it either rained hard, stormed, or hailed on us. Persistent rain is a real bummer on a backpacking trip.

We stopped again, and everyone donned rain gear; then we soldiered on. After several more hours of rain and slogging through newly formed mud, Mike and I stopped the group, set up the quickest tarp shelter we could, and got a couple of stoves going to provide warm drinks. We were worried about people getting hypothermic in the wet cold. We stood under the tarp while hail piled up like snow. Finally, the squall passed, and we got back on the trail to find a good campsite. The trail had turned into a watershed. We were not going to make our planned base-camp destination with all of the rain delays. We stopped near a high alpine meadow and set up tents just inside the forest for some measure of lightning protection.

Good thing we stopped and set up camp; a much bigger storm blew in. The thunder was deafening. And you knew it was coming before you heard a sound. The change in atmospheric pressure would suck all of the air out of the tent and then…KABOOM! I am sure that the sounds of war are indescribably worse; but in my sheltered experience, there is nothing scarier than lying in a tent at altitude on a mountainside during a thunderstorm.

Lisa, my wife and tentmate, was unhappy about the situation and verbal about her feelings. When, at one point, we distinctly heard Mike snoring in his tent nearby, she asked, "How the hell could anyone sleep in this apocalypse?"

I lovingly and supportively replied that I could—if she would just be quiet. It had been a long day.

The next day, in more rain, we made it to a base camp in a valley just above the Pecos River. Stringing up every tarp we had, as well as parts of a discarded tent we found, we erected a large rain shelter and windbreak as a living/gathering/cooking area. Everything we had was soggy. We kept a fire going (the damn drought was definitely over) and attempted to dry as much clothing as possible. There was no day hike to the local waterfall sites as planned. I spent much of the day hauling river rocks to make a rather beautiful patio and benches so we did not have to stand or sit in the mud. I bet the hikers who have followed us wonder who improved the campsite so determinedly and why.

That night, we sat around the campfire playing a round-robin game that required each person in turn to come up with and sing a song with the word "rain" in it. We also tried inventing an antirain dance and ceremony. Beth had a tremendous talent for belching on command with astonishing results. For some reason that is completely unclear to me now, she took (and won) a bet to belch the entirety of the Lord's Prayer. It was the creepiest, most sacrilegious thing I have ever witnessed. I felt as though I had experienced an exorcism—or perhaps needed to experience one right away. We made her swear never, ever to do such a thing again.

The next morning, we saw sunshine! Excited, we got ready for a day hike to a high-altitude mountain lake that mountain goats were known to frequent. Before we got to the lake, the skies turned threatening again. Disappointed, we decided to turn back to our shelter. Getting even wetter and colder did not appeal to anyone.

As we started back down, Mike stopped and said, "Is that a flying mountain goat?"

"What the hell are you talking about?" I replied. I thought that he might be getting hypothermia brain fog.

"Right there," he said, pointing.

Sure enough, a flying mountain goat was coming into view around the mountain slope a thousand feet above us. Apparently, as we discovered later, there was a Forest Service initiative to relocate and reintroduce mountain goats somewhere else. Above us was a mountain goat in big sling contraption dangling by a cable from a helicopter. Sitting on our wilderness patio that night in more rain, we theorized about the best way to catch a mountain goat and secure it in a sling. We discussed what the goat might have thought about the experience of flying. At least one member of the group wondered why we did not hail the helicopter like a cab to fly *us* out too.

Upon returning to base camp, we also discovered that a couple of people in the party, overexuberant about seeing the sunshine, had removed the rain flys from their tents—hoping the sun would dry out their belongings, maybe? But the afternoon rain we had walked through had drowned their tents, sleeping bags, and remaining clothes. Mike and I gave all of the somewhat dry clothes we had to others in the party, and that night, we had to sleep three people to each of the remaining, dry, two-person tents.

The day we walked out, there was no rain—of course. Everything on us and with us was still waterlogged, though. With everything wet, our packs seemed to weigh twice what they should have. I was known as the group pack mule, so I had a lot of Lisa's stuff, some of Beth's stuff, and no telling what else strapped to my pack. The thing had to weigh well over a hundred pounds. When we stopped for breaks, I quit taking the pack off my back because it took both Mike and me to get it back on. I would just lean up against a tree. Nonetheless, we made good time on the trail out to the van, encouraged by the promise of a real bathroom and a burger at the Dairy Queen about an hour's drive away.

At the DQ, I dropped everyone off at the door and drove around the back to park the van. I opened the door, and then discovered that my legs would not move. My leg muscles had just seized up and quit while I'd been sitting for an hour and driving. Fifteen minutes later, I finally completed the hundred-foot trek into the DQ. I had to eat standing up. As long as I kept moving a little, the legs worked fine.

What a trip! We had a great crew with good attitudes, despite all the rain. Mike, Beth, and I still laugh about that trip. We planned another trip for the next summer. Unfortunately, I do not think anyone else on that excursion ever went backpacking again. Although Lisa had been on several other trips with us, that was her last backpacking adventure. And it was a good decision. Remember the first rule: enjoy. She was game, as always, on that soggy trip, but she did not really enjoy backpacking all that much. She loves being outdoors and will gladly take a day hike, but she wants some nice amenities to return to at night. And that's fine! If you try backpacking and decide that you really don't enjoy it, there are plenty of other fun things to do instead.

Tips for the National Park Tourist Trip

So, you are not quite ready for a backcountry backpacking adventure, but you would love to spend a week in a national park; what are some tips for enjoying and navigating a more touristy national park vacation?

Lodging

The famous, grand old lodges in our national parks are fabulous in and of themselves, but getting a reservation for the summer months is difficult even a year in advance. If you do not have children in tow and are not limited to the crowded, high-season, summer months, then try planning a trip in May or September (or whatever the off-season for that particular park is). You will be rolling the dice a bit with the weather—spring and fall can mean beautiful, eighty-degree days or so much snow and cold that half of the roads in the park are closed—but you probably can get a reservation at one of the cool, old lodges. You will also feel like you have the park to yourself because you will be dealing with one-tenth of the peak-season crowds.

If your vacation happens during the peak-season rush, get creative with lodging. Make your lodging part of the adventure. Some Internet searching will show you a wide variety of options. Get out of hotel mode. Did you really decide to visit a national park in order to stay at a nondescript hotel? Here are options to consider:

- If several families are going on the trip and sharing costs, look on a wide variety of Internet sites for vacation homes to rent. On a multiple-family trip to Yosemite, we found an unbelievable "log cabin" at Bass Lake. This place had to be a several-million-dollar property. It slept ten to twelve in beds in four separate rooms. There was also a tepee in the backyard with a queen-sized bed. The kitchen and balconies were to die for. The cost was nearly three thousand dollars for a week, but with four families pitching in, it worked out to less than the cost of a mediocre hotel room per person. In Glacier, we had the same experience—a house on the Flathead River only a couple of miles from the park entrance was amazing and affordable.
- Try the "glamping" trend. Glacier National Park (and several other parks) have campgrounds just outside the entrance where you can stay in large tents with queen-sized beds and dressers and tables. You will have to walk to a nice, shared, bathroom and shower complex. The rates are reasonable—certainly less than a stay in a hotel or lodge. Or, stay at one of the many mom-and-pop cabin businesses surrounding our parks.
- Plan to rent a space in, or near, the park to pitch your tent. At Yellowstone, Sealock and I reserved a place with a cooking grill and a bear box for food storage inside the park for our arrival night. Across the gravel road was a great meadow for stargazing and wildlife watching. No one was near us. The cost was nearly nothing. Between Yellowstone and Grand Teton, in the Flagg Ranch area, there all kinds of tent-space places that you can reserve. They offer quick access to either park. The common restroom and shower facilities are well kept. Restaurant, gas, and supply stores are nearby. The cost is minimal.
- If you are flexible and willing to roll without a fixed plan, some parks (such as Glacier National Park) have campsites available inside the park. Unfortunately, you cannot make reservations for

these spaces. You show up, drive around, and claim an empty spot on a first come, first served basis. Again, you will have access to a serviceable and clean bathroom and shower facility. We have had good luck with these kinds of arrangements, and the twenty-dollar-a-night cost is hard to beat. But you have to be ready to move to plan *B* or *C* at the last moment if the sites are full.

Even if you choose to sleep at a more adventuresome option, I would still encourage you to visit the grand old lodges. They are destinations in their own right. You can still get dinner reservations if you are willing to eat at 5:00 p.m. or so. Or you can just drop by, wander around, and hang at the bar for a while.

Do try to stay as close to a national park entrance as possible; there is no sense in adding to your (already significant) driving time.

Roads and Driving Times

Most national parks are quite big, and you will spend a significant part of your time just driving from place to place. Distances are deceiving. What reads as twenty miles from point *A* to point *B* on a map will likely take you an hour. You only have one lane. You are probably in the mountains. Maybe a few bison decided to walk down the road and are backing up traffic for miles. The only time that construction crews can work on the roads is exactly when half a million tourists are driving through the park. These roads are stunning engineering feats with astonishing views, but they are not interstate freeways. Plan accordingly.

Get Going Early! Reset Your Daily Clock

National parks are crowded in the peak summer season. Yellowstone, for example, will see better than a million visitors per month in June, July, and August. Most people on vacation, however, cannot get their acts together early in the morning. To beat the lines at the park entrance, on the roads, and at popular attractions, start your day as early as possible—like witness-the-sunrise early. Get up, eat a good breakfast, and get going as early as you can to beat the lines at the park entrance and on the roads.

Have a Daily Plan

Drive to the place you want to see that is the farthest from your starting point; then, work your way back to your lodging place with stops of interest along the way. Pack a lunch, snacks, and plenty of water. Plan to picnic in the car or at an attraction. Otherwise, you'll waste a couple of hours in some concessions line. Eat your lunch early (at elevenish) so you can hit a few popular attractions while the crowds are in line looking for lunch. Plan to eat dinner at five or so (again to beat the lines and crowds). Then you have a long summer evening free to explore more of the park while the crowds diminish, or you can settle in for an early, relaxing evening. Plan the next day with an early start. Have a plan, but always be ready and willing to adapt the plan when interesting opportunities or circumstances intervene.

Buy an Annual Pass

Get the card that gets your entire carload of people into any park for a year. Eighty dollars instead of thirty dollars is not a big deal. It's not a lot more money than the one time entrance fee, and you will be supporting the National Park Service. You can use the card for admission to any national park or national monument for an entire year.

Consider Using the Bus Service

Some national parks have excellent bus services and routes within the park. Park your car easily at a bus center and start riding. No more trolling for parking spaces. Meet some interesting people. Actually look around instead of driving. Or, if you are like Sealock, just fall asleep while someone else drives.

Take a Day Hike

Only a small fraction of 1 percent of people visiting a national park go backpacking. There are no reliable statistics for day hiking, but personal experience tells me that an astonishingly small percentage of people walk more than a mile or two in our national parks. If you want to truly experience the wild in our parks, then plan on a morning or afternoon hike of three to five miles (round trip). Or, plan a longer hike for most of a day. The longer the hike, the fewer people you will see.

Check Out the Ranger Programs

Look for posted schedules of ranger talks, programs, and guided tours. At Badlands National Park in South Dakota, I sat with a few people in a natural amphitheater and watched the International Space Station move, on schedule, across the sky from horizon to horizon. We spent the rest of the evening identifying constellations and galaxies that could be seen with the naked eye. In Hawaii, the rangers set up telescopes that brought into focus stunning, colorful nebulae and galaxies of various shapes. In Utah, I talked to a guest speaker who helped to design one of the Mars rovers—he even brought a cool model. Talks about local history, biology, wildlife, geology, and paleontology are common. Most of these activities are free.

At the stately Lodge at Crater Lake National Park in Oregon, Lisa and I listened to a ranger talk about bears. Afterward, the ranger asked for questions. No one in the small crowd said anything. So I raised my hand.

"Where do you get those distinctive hats that park service rangers wear?" I asked. The question was off the subject, perhaps, but I really wanted to know. The ranger was not amused. She launched into a long answer about how distinctive the hats were and how they were made specially for the park service, and she intimated that it might be against federal law for anyone else even to try to buy such a hat.

When I got home, I told that story to Mike. Somehow, he and my friends found the place in Georgia that specially makes ranger hats and ordered me one for my birthday that year. It was the best birthday present ever—except that it did not fit my head. Apparently, I have a gigantic head for a guy my size. So, we had to go through the process of returning the custom-made hat for a larger size. The hat now hangs on the wall in my office, right next to my collection of made-on-the-trail walking sticks.

Resolutions and Knots

Many years ago, after finishing college and graduate school, I wanted to be intentional about lifelong learning. Of course, all kinds of regular habits will help a person to develop that practice: reading, being curious and inquisitive, meeting and befriending interesting people, trying new things, and rebelling enough to avoid small, boxed-in world views.

One habit I adopted was making a New Year's resolution to invest the effort and time to learn about a topic of interest and to practice doing that thing. Very early on, one of those resolutions was to learn about backpacking. Obviously, that resolution turned into a lifelong love.

Over the years, other resolutions have turned into seriously fun hobbies, such as paleontology and fossil hunting. I am glad that I learned something about all of the topics and activities that I landed on, even the ones that did not stick. Some, like scuba diving, I still practice occasionally when the opportunity arises.

My resolution this year was to practice writing and to write and publish a book…this book. If you enjoyed this book and found it useful, please suggest the book to your friends! Unlike many of today's authors, I am not upselling anyone, collecting e-mails, or trying to become famous for business purposes. I simply love the outdoors and want to encourage more people to get out there. I enjoyed this project, and I hope you and your friends will enjoy the book.

Next year, I think I should learn to tie proper knots. For all of my experience outdoors and around boats, I stink at knots. Any Cub Scout can make knots much better than I can. I am tired of being embarrassed—and pretending to be busy doing some other task—while someone else makes a necessary knot. Pitiful. I hope that by the time you are reading this book, I have become some kind of zen knot master. Really, how hard can it be to learn how to tie proper knots?

New Year or not, I hope you resolve to do two things after reading this book. First, I hope you decide to get outdoors more to enjoy and explore the natural world around you. Second, I hope you will discover all kinds of interesting things on your walks and then decide to learn more about them. In no time, you will be an enthusiast about things you never even thought about before.

You probably noticed that there are no pictures in this book. I have thousands of pictures of amazing adventures and places, but a photo never does the real thing justice. You really have to be there. So, get out there and see for yourself. Happy trails to you!

AFTERWORD: ENVIRONMENT

Spend some time in any of America's designated wilderness areas, and you will undoubtedly develop a keener interest in protecting and preserving those lands for generations to come. Such lands belong to the American people—to you and me. Be a good steward. Your advocacy and support will always be needed to keep the greedy hands of politicians (of every ilk) and their puppeteers off your shared lands and the national inheritance of your children's children's children.

If you have never seen Ken Burns's historical documentary *The National Parks: America's Best Idea*, then you should stop right now and order the series. The history of the parks, presented in the context of American history and American ideals and against the backdrop of conflicts between industry and early conservation movements, is fascinating, compelling, and inspiring.

Theodore Roosevelt, a Republican, was not only one of our greatest presidents, but he was also the greatest political advocate for preserving the American wilderness. His passion and foresight began our national park system, and to conserve those lands he had to fight the overreach of the industrialists of his time. Why was Teddy Roosevelt such a great conservationist? Simply because he actually spent time in the backcountry of America. He lived for a while near what is now Theodore Roosevelt National Park in North Dakota. He camped in places such as Yellowstone. Even while president, he camped with John Muir in Yosemite. If you spend some time in these kinds of places, you will come home with a different perspective, too.

Times change. Political parties have flipped ideologies several times in the course of America's history. They seem to alter direction with every cultural swing, and the politicians themselves change with every new poll. I don't give a flip about Republicans or Democrats, nor do I trust either party's required-for-membership, check-your-brain-at-the-door, groupthink orthodoxy. I don't join cults. I value actual information and scientific data. I value independent thinking and practical solutions. I do not subscribe to the nonsense that political beliefs, myths, or slogans magically or conveniently alter the fundamental physical laws of the universe. I do know that if money and political clout align when the public is distracted, then almost any politician will happily destroy any American wilderness treasure—or the environment, in general—for his or her own short-term gain.

As I write in 2017, the current Republican regime is on a scorched-earth rampage to eviscerate the Environmental Protection Agency and the National Oceanic and Atmospheric Administration in order to throttle all scientific environmental inquiry, squash data, and roll back four decades of somewhat better environmental stewardship—all with the grand vision of turning America into an industry-cozy and heavily polluted country like China. Under this political leadership, the EPA has been recast as the Environmental Polluting Agency with the new mission of ensuring that no business will ever be inconvenienced by any environmental, pollution, public health, or public safety concern.

The only natural resources that this current crop of Republicans values are those that can be sold to the highest bidder. Government, actual facts, and intelligent regulations are out of fashion right now. Where is a real Republican such as Theodore Roosevelt when you need one? Please remember these "stewards" who rushed to set up this all-you-can-eat-as-fast-as-you-can buffet when the bill comes due and we have to try to clean up the mess again.

Who knows what the politics of tomorrow will bring? I don't care at all about the fortunes of the red team or the blue team, but I do care very much about our American wilderness and our environment. Regardless of who is throwing the party in Washington, DC, or in your state, *your* consistent vigilance, voice, support, and activism will be needed if we are to keep the American wilderness—and the environment—intact.

ABOUT THE AUTHOR

Mick Tune holds degrees from Vanderbilt University and Brite Divinity School. An avid lover of the outdoors, Mick has enjoyed hiking, back-packing, and fossil hunting for more than three decades. He currently lives in Heath, Texas, with his wife of thirty-five years.

Made in the USA
Columbia, SC
27 September 2017